John Comfort Fillmore

Pianoforte Music

Its History, with Biographical Sketches and Critical Estimates of its ...

John Comfort Fillmore

Pianoforte Music
Its History, with Biographical Sketches and Critical Estimates of its ...

ISBN/EAN: 9783744779111

Printed in Europe, USA, Canada, Australia, Japan

Cover: Foto ©Thomas Meinert / pixelio.de

More available books at **www.hansebooks.com**

PIANOFORTE MUSIC:

ITS HISTORY, WITH BIOGRAPHICAL SKETCHES AND CRITICAL ESTIMATES OF ITS GREATEST MASTERS.

BY

JOHN COMFORT FILLMORE.

PHILADELPHIA:
THEODORE PRESSER,
1708 CHESTNUT STREET.
1896.

COPYRIGHT 1883
TOWNSEND MAC COUN,
CHICAGO.

PREFACE.

IN entering a field hitherto unoccupied by any English-speaking writer, the author of this book has had in view the following objects:

To discriminate clearly the natural epochs into which the history of pianoforte music divides; to give a lucid statement and exposition of the principles of composition which have governed and determined the creative activity of those epochs; to trace the development of these principles as manifested in the phenomena of composition, and to point out the relation of the work of each epoch to what preceded and what followed it; to call attention to the great epoch-making composers whose work furnishes the chief examples of those characteristic principles; to give a clear and discriminating account of their work, a trustworthy estimate of their relative rank and place in history, and to furnish biographical sketches of them sufficiently full to give general readers a not inadequate notion of the men and their lives; to notice the work and lives of minor composers and performers with as much fullness as the limits of the book would permit; to trace the development of the technic of the pianoforte; to give a sufficient account of the instruments which preceded the pianoforte, and of their relation to that instrument.

How far he has succeeded in his aims he leaves to the judgment of his readers. But whatever shortcomings may be discovered in his work, the attempt is one which he believes requires no apology. The number of those who are strongly interested in the best pianoforte music is already large and is rapidly increasing. To all such, and especially to those who, like the author, are engaged in teaching the pianoforte, a connected account of the course of development of that music and of the composers who were instrumental in that development, can not fail to be welcome.

Of the subjects here expounded, "The Content of Music" and "The Classic and Romantic" certainly deserve much more attention than they have hitherto received, and it is hoped that the present exposition will be found valuable. The biographical sketch of Chopin will be found more complete and accurate than any heretofore published in English, and the other biographies and critical estimates are at least fresh, and express the author's own judgments.

The work has been a labor of love, and the author

can find no better wish for those who may do him the honor to be his readers, than that they may find the perusal of his work as interesting and profitable as the composition of it, and the necessary preparation for that composition, have been to himself. With this wish, and the sincere hope that his work may not only give useful information, but prove a helpful stimulus to the highest musical and intellectual life, he offers it to the public.

J. C. F.

MILWAUKEE, WIS., March 27 1883.

NOTE.—The author takes this opportunity to acknowledge his obligations to numerous friends, and especially to Professors J. M. Geery, of Ripon College, W. S. B. Mathews, of Chicago, and Librarian Linderfelt, of the Milwaukee Public Library, for valuable suggestions, criticism and assistance.

PREFACE TO FOURTH EDITION.

The author has felt called upon to make a few additions to the list of minor composers and concert pianists (all Americans) of the present time. He has made a very few verbal changes in the book and has added questions at the end of the chapters, hoping thereby to increase its usefulness. Beyond these improvements he sees no way of bettering his work at present. He takes occasion once more to express his thanks to the musical public for its approval of his efforts.

MILWAUKEE, *October, 1888.*

CONSPECTUS.

INTRODUCTION.

THE PIANOFORTE AND ITS IMMEDIATE PRECURSORS, THE HARPSICHORD AND THE CLAVICHORD.

PART I.

THE FIRST CLASSICAL PERIOD.

CHAPTER I.—POLYPHONIC MUSIC.

CHAPTER II.—THE THREE GREATEST COMPOSERS OF POLYPHONIC MUSIC FOR THE HARPSICHORD : J. S. BACH, G. F. HAENDEL, D. SCARLATTI.

PART II.

THE SECOND CLASSICAL PERIOD.

A. THE EPOCH OF THE DEVELOPMENT OF THE SONATA-FORM.

CHAPTER III.—MONOPHONIC MUSIC—FORM—THE SONATA-FORM.

CHAPTER IV.—THE THREE COMPOSERS WHO DEVELOPED THE SONATA-FORM TO ITS LOGICAL LIMITS : C. P. E. BACH, JOSEPH HAYDN, W. A. MOZART.

B. THE EPOCH OF THE PREDOMINANCE OF CONTENT IN THE SONATA.

CHAPTER V.—THE CONTENT OF MUSIC.

CHAPTER VI.—L. VAN BEETHOVEN : THE COMPOSER WHO EMBODIED IN THE SONATA THE NOBLEST POSSIBLE CONTENT AND RAISED IT TO THE HIGHEST SIGNIFICANCE AS A WORK OF ART.

C. THE TRANSITION FROM THE CLASSIC TO THE ROMANTIC PERIOD.

CHAPTER VII.—THE CLASSIC AND THE ROMANTIC IN MUSIC.

CHAPTER VIII.—BEETHOVEN'S TWO GREATEST CONTEMPORARIES IN THE DOMAIN OF PIANOFORTE MUSIC: C. M. VON WEBER AND FRANZ SCHUBERT.

PART III.

THE ROMANTIC PERIOD.

CHAPTER IX.—MENDELSSOHN, CHOPIN AND SCHUMANN.

PART IV

THE DEVELOPMENT OF PIANOFORTE TECHNIC.

CHAPTER X.—THE TECHNIC OF THE FIRST CLASSICAL PERIOD.

CHAPTER XI.—THE TECHNIC OF THE SECOND CLASSICAL PERIOD.

CHAPTER XII.—THE TECHNIC OF THE TRANSITION PERIOD.

CHAPTER XIII.—THE TECHNIC OF THE ROMANTIC PERIOD.

PART V.

MINOR COMPOSERS AND VIRTUOSI OF THE DIFFERENT EPOCHS.

CHAPTER XIV.—A. THE EPOCH OF POLYPHONIC MUSIC.
    B. THE EPOCH OF THE SONATA.
    C. THE CONTEMPORARIES OF THE ROMANTICISTS AND THEIR SUCCESSORS, TO THE PRESENT.

HISTORY OF PIANOFORTE MUSIC.

INTRODUCTION.

THE PIANOFORTE AND ITS PRECURSORS, THE CLAVI-
CHORD AND THE HARPSICHORD.

The pianoforte* is an instrument too well known to require description here. Its characteristic peculiarity, as distinguished from the instruments from which it was derived, the harpsichord and the clavichord, is that the tone produced from its strings can be made soft or loud at the pleasure of the performer. The means by which these effects are produced consist in hammers connected with the keys, and so arranged that the performer can, by graduating his touch, make them strike the strings with varying degrees of force, with the effect of eliciting every degree of sonority of which the strings are capable.

INTRODUCTION.
The Pianoforte.

The pianoforte was invented in Italy, at the beginning of the eighteenth century. The first pianofortes of which we have any authentic information were made in Florence, by Bartholomew Cristofori,

Invented in Italy about 1700.

---

*The name "pianoforte" is a compound of two Italian words, *piano*, soft, and *forte*, loud. It means, therefore, etymologically, a "soft-loud."

INTRODUCTION.

in 1709. These instruments were the result of efforts to improve the harpsichord, so as to make it capable of producing tones of various degrees of power. This need was everywhere felt, and other makers of harpsichords, in other countries, were also engaged in attempting to solve this problem. The harpsichord and clavichord had this in common with the pianoforte; they had metallic strings, stretched horizontally in a frame over a sounding board, and were played by means of keys. But the strings of the harpsichord were *snapped*, by means of crow's quills, and those of the clavichord were set in vibration by means of a *push* from a small brass wedge or "tangent," set in the end of the keys. This latter instrument already had some capability of gradations of power, and for this reason it was a favorite with the best musicians. It required great delicacy of touch, and in the hands of a master was, within certain limits, a very expressive instrument. But strings vibrated in this manner were necessarily thin and light, and produced only soft and delicate tones.

The Harpsichord and Clavichord.

Their tones weak.

The harpsichord also had light strings, and its tones were weak. It was not only impossible to produce much *variation* in the power of the tone, but no powerful tone could be obtained from any string, whether light or heavy, by any such methods of producing vibration. Heavy strings, especially, must be *struck*, not snapped nor pushed, in order to produce their maximum of tone; and it was in the direction of heavy strings and a larger sounding board that progress was to be made toward an increase of sonority, after the means had been found of producing the greatest amount of tone of which the lighter strings were capable, as well as of varying their power.

In the early part of the last century, then, the clavichord and harpsichord had reached the limit of their development, and musicians and instrument makers were anxiously striving to secure results of which these instruments were intrinsically incapable. But, though Cristofori, and others of his contemporaries and immediate succcessors, hit on the right principle, the first crude applications of it were not immediately successful. The new instruments did not find favor with players for a long time. This was partly because of the still remaining defects of their construction, for much time was required to perfect the complicated action of the pianoforte so as to secure promptness, delicacy and power of touch, to damp the strings properly, to remove the hammer from the string as soon as it had struck, and have it in readiness for an instant repetition of the stroke. It was also partly due, perhaps, to the fact that players accustomed to the older instruments could not readily find themselves at home with the new mechanism, and preferred that with which they were familiar. At any rate, so great a musician and player as J. S. Bach, condemned the Silbermann pianofortes shown him in 1726, as being heavy in touch, and weak in the treble; his son, C. P. E. Bach, is said always to have preferred the

New results sought.

Mechanical results to be attained.

Introduction.

clavichord, and even Mozart, to the end of his life, was a harpsichord player, rather than a pianist.

But toward the end of the century, great improvements were made in the construction of the pianoforte; the number of compositions specially calculated for the capabilities of the instrument had greatly increased; the younger musicians had became familiar with its manipulation; and by the beginning of the present century, the clavichord and harpsichord were driven forever out of use.

The Spinet and Virginals.

In closing this brief sketch, it remains to give a passing glance at two other instruments, the *spinet* and *virginals*. Concerning these it is only necessary to say that they were merely varieties of the harpsichord, differing from it only in shape and size, but not in principle, much as square and upright pianofortes differ from a concert grand, which is shaped like the old harpsichords.

A full account of all these instruments is to be found in Grove's Dictionary of Music and Musicians.

PART FIRST.
THE FIRST CLASSICAL PERIOD.
1700–1750.

CHAPTER I.

POLYPHONIC MUSIC.

Melody is a *series* or *succession* of tones rhythmically ordered.

Harmony is a *combination* of tones heard simultaneously.

Counterpoint is the art of writing two or more melodies to proceed simultaneously. Music thus written is called "*contrapuntal*," or "*polyphonic*." The latter term means "many-voiced." In polyphonic music, harmony is an incidental result of the simultaneous progression of the voices.

"*Monophonic*" or "*homophonic*"* music has only one principal melody. This is usually accompanied by chords, more or less full, either in their simple form, or broken up into arpeggios. Sometimes, however, other subordinate melodies form the accompaniment, to a greater or less extent. This is especially true of the bass, which often is a well-defined melody, but is never, in this style of music, quite equal in importance and interest to the principal melody. Sometimes, indeed, the principal melody is given to the bass, the harmonic accompaniment being above it.

CHAP. 1.
Definition of Terms.

---

*The present writer has chosen the term "monophonic" ("one-voiced"), as representing more accurately the fact that music in this style has only one prominent melody at any given point. Many German writers prefer the term "homophonic."

In the monophonic style of composition, harmony is no longer an *accident*, so to speak, but the chords, in their successions and relations, exist independent of any interweaving of separate melodic parts.

Beginnings of Modern Music.

The beginnings of our modern music, in the early Christian church, were monophonic in the strictest sense. The congregations sang their hymns in unison, without any accompaniment. Afterwards, singers and composers began to accompany this melody with one or more independent melodies, in tones of the *same* length as those of the original melody, or *cantus firmus*, as it was called. This was the beginning of *counterpoint*, "*punctum contra punctum*," point against point. At that time there were no notes; points were used instead. We should say note against note. Certain monks of the middle ages cultivated this science; sought to determine what intervals might be admissible; and gradually developed their art to a high pitch of perfection. The separate melodies gradually became more and more florid, the number of them was increased, until, at last, compositions were written in as many as *thirty-six* real parts. Of course, these extremely complicated webs of tone were nearly or quite unintelligible to most musicians, and wholly so to amateurs. But they were masterpieces of ingenuity, and the interest in counterpoint which produced them, had developed consummate skill in the management of simultaneously progressing voice-parts.

Early Counterpoint.

The *technic* of composition in this first great

style (the polyphonic) was developed through the enthusiastic labors of composers, monks, theorists and pedants, among whom there appeared, now and then, a man of genuine creative genius. Among these ought especially to be mentioned ORLANDUS LASSUS, (1530 (?)–1594) a Netherlander, whose most important work was done in Munich, and GIOVANNI PIERLIUGI DI PALESTRINA (1524–1594), a Roman church composer, in whom the contrapuntal art previous to Sebastian Bach found its culmination.

The technic of Composition developed.

At first, the efforts of contrapuntists were directed solely toward the discovery of intervals pleasing to the ear, and combining melodies so as to produce agreeable effects at every point. Then came the effort to enhance the effect of consonances by the judicious use of dissonances. This resulted in making the parts more smooth and flowing in their movement. But, as the separate melodies began to be more and more florid, the need of some means of securing *unity* was felt. A complicated web of interwoven melodies, having no elements in common, and no bond of union except consonance in their intervals would be nearly or quite unintelligible. The means by which unity was secured was *Imitation*.

The pleasing in sensation sought first.

Of Imitation there are two principal kinds, the *Strict* and the *Free*.

The simplest form of Strict Imitation is the *Canon*. In this form of composition, after one melody has proceeded alone for one or more measures, another part (or "voice") begins the same melody, and con-

Strict Imitation

tinues it, in strict imitation, at the interval of an octave (or perhaps some other interval), until the final cadence of the first melody is reached, when the second melody is modified to suit the requirements of the close, and both come to an end together. Of course, in the invention of the first melody regard must be had to the imitation which is to progress with it. This requires much ingenuity and skill. There are also canons in three, four, or more parts; and many curious and ingenious kinds of canons, which can not here be described.

The Fugue.

The most elaborate of the forms of Strict Imitation is the *Fugue*. This is the culmination of the strict polyphonic style, both in respect of technical requirements, of beauty, and expressive power. A fugue may be written in two, three, four, five or more parts. Some one of the parts starts with a short, well-defined melody, which is the "*subject*" of the fugue. Then another voice replies with an imitation of this subject, in the key of the dominant. This imitation is called the "*answer.*" The first part accompanies the answer by a new melodic phrase, so contrived as to contrast with the original phrase and serve as a foil to it. This is called the "*counter subject.*" If the fugue is in two parts only, when the answer is completed by the second part, the "*exposition*" of the fugue is said to be complete. Then follows an *interlude* or *episode*, in which fragments of the subject and counter subject are used as imitations. This episode leads to the second entry of the subject, which commonly takes place in reverse

The Fugue in two-voice parts.

order to the exposition; *i. e.*, if the exposition began with the soprano and the bass answered it, the bass now leads with the subject and the soprano follows with the answer. After this comes another episode, and then a "*stretto,*" where the answer enters before the subject has finished. The whole is closed with a "*coda,*" more or less elaborate.

This is the simplest outline of the fugue form. When the fugue is written for three, four or more voices, there are often more than three entries of the subject and answer in all the parts. After the exposition, or first complete entry of all the voices, the order of entrance and the modulations into different keys are left to the imagination and skill of the composer. So are the length and richness of the interludes, and the greater or less elaboration of the coda. The stretto is sometimes a strict canon. The counter subject is often so constructed as to go in *double* counterpoint with the subject; that is, is so contrived that the lower of them may be transposed an octave higher, or the higher an octave lower, and the relations of the two still be correct and satisfactory. There are fugues with two, three, four and more subjects.

Free Imitation occurs when the imitations of a given subject or "*motive*" take place without any exact following of the original order of intervals, and not in accordance with any fixed rule as to their number, or the order of their entrance. The old compositions in this style were Preludes, Inventions, Fantasias, Toccatas, Sonatas, and various forms of dance music. Most of the compositions passing under these names were polyphonic.

The sonata form will be considered further on. The *Suite* was a series of dance tunes, often introduced by a prelude. They were invariably all in the same key, and were so arranged as to contrast with one another in *tempo*. The first dance was commonly moderately fast; the second very rapid, the third slow and stately, the fourth and perhaps the fifth less slow, but still majestic and dignified, and the last a lively, rollicking jig.

The following examples are recommended to students. J. S. Bach, "Two-part and Three-part Inventions," "Das Wohltemperirte Clavier" (The Well-Tempered Clavichord), a collection of forty-eight preludes and fugues in all the keys; English and French Suites and Partitas. Haendel,* sixteen Suites, Leçons, Pieces, Fugues, Fuguettes. D. Scarlatti, eighteen pieces (Buelow). All these can be obtained in the cheap but excellent edition of C. F. Peters in Leipzig. There is also a set of pieces by Scarlatti, edited by Louis Koehler, and published by Julius Schuberth & Co., Leipzig.

The polyphonic music was first written for voices, and for the service of the church. Afterwards secular music, (madrigals, etc.) came into vogue. When the organ and other keyed instruments had been invented, they were at first used for accompani-

---

*For typographical reasons the e is used in this and all other cases instead of the umlaut.

ments to vocal music. From this it was an easy step to transfer the vocal forms to separate instrumental performances, and this naturally led to independent composition for these instruments. The most elaborate and masterly fugues are those of J. S. Bach, for the organ and clavichord. For these instruments the polyphonic music was written, and with the year of Bach's death, 1750, this first classical period may be said to have closed. Its significance to us lies in the fact that all its treasures are still available for the pianoforte, which has supplanted the harpsichord and clavichord, and that a knowledge of it is indispensable to every pianist.

CHAPTER II.

THE THREE GREATEST COMPOSERS OF POLYPHONIC MUSIC FOR THE HARPSICHORD:

JOHANN SEBASTIAN BACH, 1685-1750.
GEORGE FREDERICK HAENDEL, 1685-1759.
DOMENICO SCARLATTI, 1683-1757.

CHAP. II.
J. S. Bach.

By far the most important of all composers for the harpsichord was John Sebastian Bach. He was the most distinguished representative of a numerous family of musicians, who lived in Eisenach and its neighboring towns for some two centuries. They were a simple, honest, straightforward, high-minded race; they lived quiet domestic lives, and devoted themselves to their art, with a simplicity of character, and an elevation of purpose, which always secured them the respect and love of their fellow-townsmen. The subject of this sketch was born in Eisenach, March 21, 1685. He received his first lessons from his father, beginning with the violin. But losing both his parents before he was ten years old, he went to live with his older brother, Johann Christoph, organist at Ohrdruff. With him he began lessons on the clavichord. He made remarkable progress, and speedily gave evidence of the gifts which were by and by to raise him to the highest pinnacle of fame.

Life and education at his brother's.

His brother seems to have repressed rather than encouraged the impulses of the child's genius. He not only refused him the use of his own collection of music, by the best masters of the time, but after the boy had surreptitiously obtained the book, and laboriously copied the whole, by moonlight, this hard-hearted and unappreciative teacher took the well-earned and dearly-prized copy away from him. At the age of fifteen, he was sent away to Lueneburg to school, and entered the choir, in which his services paid for his school tuition, including vocal and instrumental music. He made rapid progress in playing the organ and harpsichord, and improved every opportunity to hear the best performers of Lueneburg and the neighboring town of Hamburg. He was also greatly influenced and inspired by the performances of the duke's orchestra at Celle, a band at that time made up largely of Frenchmen, and playing mostly French music.

He remained at Lueneburg three years. At the end of that time he entered an orchestra at Weimar, and soon after became organist at Arnstadt. Here he studied and practiced with the utmost diligence and zeal, striving to perfect himself, both in playing, and in theory and composition. In 1705 he spent three months at Luebeck, for the purpose of hearing the celebrated organist, Buxtehude, and of becoming acquainted with him.

Bach's reputation as an organist was now beginning to spread. He received several offers of situations, and in 1707 he accepted an organist's post at Muehlhausen in Thueringen, but left it in 1708, when he was twenty-three years old, to become court or-

CHAP. II.
Becomes Court organist.

ganist in Weimar. Here he remained nine years, during which time he won acknowledged rank as first of organists and organ composers. He wrote here most of his greatest works for the organ. He made annual concert-tours, playing both the organ and clavichord, and won an extended reputation as a master of the highest rank.

In 1717, he accepted the appointment of conductor at Coethen, and now for five years devoted himself mainly to composing, and directing public performances of chamber music. But in 1723, he was appointed cantor at the St. Thomas school at Leipzig, and also organist and director of music in the two principal churches. Here he remained until his death, July 28, 1750, writing music for his choir for almost every service; chorals, motets, cantatas, and great works for the festivals of the church, among them one High Mass, and his immortal Passion Music.

Removes to Leipzig.

For the rest, he lived a quiet, retired life, devoting himself, not only to his musical labors, but to the education of his numerous children, of whom he had twenty, by two marriages. The most notable incident which broke the monotony of his daily routine, was a visit to Frederick the Great, in 1747. Bach's son Emanuel was Frederick's principal court-musician. The king, who was a lover of music, invited the father to visit him, and treated him with greatest respect and consideration. As usual, Bach's playing and his wonderful skill in improvising on given themes, excited the strongest admiration.

Visits Frederick the Great.

Soon after this he became blind, and continued so for the short remainder of his life. His death occurred from a fit of apoplexy, July 28, 1750.

Death.

Bach was one of the world's great creative minds; an original genius of the highest order; a most consummate master of the art of musical composition as understood in his day, and he had no superior in playing the harpsichord and clavichord. All the resources and capabilities of these instruments he thoroughly understood. He was, it is true, very much more than a master of the harpsichord; he was the greatest organist of his time, and his organ compositions are the noblest and most significant the world has yet known. He was a teacher and choir-leader, and a very large part of his mental activity was spent in the production of church music, of which he has left behind an immense amount,— hundreds of cantatas, motets, chorals, a great Mass in B minor, five separate settings of the Passion of our Lord as given in the gospels, of which that stupendous work, the Passion Music according to St. Matthew, will forever remain one of the great monuments of Protestant religious art. But though he composed so much for chorus, organ and orchestra, besides chamber music, he nevertheless wrote a very large number of compositions for the harpsichord.

Bach's rank.

Many of these works are of permanent value from their nobility and beauty of style and their intrinsic emotional significance, and all are characterized by high intellectual qualities, and consummate musicianship. Moreover, although the instruments for

His works for the Harpsichord.

CHAP. II.

His influence on the Romanticists.

His stimulating quality.

which they were written have become totally obsolete, the style, and even the technic of these compositions is such, that whoever wishes to take a high rank as a pianist, must devote to them the most earnest and diligent study. This is doubly true if the pianist aims beyond mere technic, at high artistic qualities and musicianship. Said Robert Schumann, "Make the 'Well Tempered Clavichord' your daily bread; then you will surely become a thorough musician." This advice, coming from a writer apparently as far removed as possible from the manner and style of Bach, is highly significant. Chopin and Mendelssohn, who, with Schumann, made the Modern Romantic School of pianoforte writing, were diligent students of Bach, and drew a large part of their inspiration from him. These facts may help to show us how immensely important Bach's influence has been, and still is. The secret of this influence lies partly in the profound originality, and the inspired quality of Bach's genius, and partly in the unsurpassed intellectual grasp and power by which his works are everywhere characterized. The study of a Bach fugue is an intellectual exercise of the most salutary kind; an exercise, the severity of whose demands on mental concentration and on the power of sustained thinking, constitutes a most valuable means of intellectual discipline. There is no keener intellectual pleasure than these works afford, to him who has mastered them.

Bach's instrumental works are the culmination of the polyphonic or contrapuntal style. Up to his time this was the prevalent manner of writing, and almost the only one cultivated by musicians. The monophonic style, indeed, had already a beginning. Opera airs and folk songs had been transferred to the keyed instruments; some dance music also had come to be written in this style. But the aim of all composers was to write good counterpoint, and that in the strict style, canons and fugues. Freer forms were also used, as described in the preceding chapter, which gave more scope to the fancy of the composer. Though founded on the fugal style, they often showed a reaching out after a freer, more elastic and flexible means of emotional expression than was to be found in the comparatively stiff formality of the strict mode of writing. One, especially, of these works, the Chromatic Fantasia of Bach, is a distinct prophecy of the Romantic School, which was to appear a hundred years later.

GEORGE FREDERICK HAENDEL (commonly called in England Handel), was born in Halle, Feb. 23, 1685. His family was not musical, and whence he obtained his musical gifts it is not easy to determine. But gifts he had, which were not to be repressed. His father was a physician, who despised all art and artists, and even went to the extreme of keeping his son from school, lest he should there learn something of music. But the boy learned somehow, in spite of his father. He used to practice on an old spinet, with muffled strings, which, with somebody's connivance, he had hidden in the garret, and by the time he was seven years old, had become no mean performer. At this time his whole future career was decided by the interference of the Duke of Saxe-Weissenfels. The child had accompanied his father on a visit to Weissenfels, had managed to obtain access to the organ in the duke's chapel, and had given such surprising proofs of genius that the duke strongly urged upon doctor Haendel the wisdom of humoring his son's bent.

Lessons with Zachau.

He was now placed under the tuition of Zachau, organist of the cathedral at Halle, and took lessons on the organ, harpsichord, violin and oboe, and in counterpoint, canon, fugue, and all the forms of composition then practiced. He wrote a motet every week during the three years he remained with Zachau. His master then confessed that he could teach him nothing more. The ten-year old boy was sent to Berlin, where he made some valuable musical acquaintances, and astonished every one by his surprising improvisations on the organ and harpsichord.

He soon returned to Halle, and spent some years in study and composition, copying large quantities of the best music then known. His father died, and left George and his mother poor. So the boy set to work to support them both. In 1703, he went to Hamburg and entered the orchestra of the German opera-house, as a violin player. He amused himself a short time by pretending to be very ignorant, but happening to take the leader's place at the harpsichord one day, in the absence of the regular conductor, he displayed such ability as at once

Enters the Hamburg opera orchestra.

placed him permanently in that position. He remained here three years, and composed his first three operas, besides other compositions. The success of these, his pay at the theater, and what he had earned by giving lessons, had enabled him to lay up a considerable sum, beyond what was required to support himself and his mother. So he determined to make a musical pilgrimage to Italy, the country which had been the field of labor of some of the greatest of the Netherland contrapuntists, where the ancient contrapuntal style of Catholic church music had culminated in Palestrina, where the opera had first been called into existence,—the country whose leadership in music was still unquestioned.

He spent three years in the great musical centers of Italy, Rome, Venice, Naples and Florence. He composed successful operas, church music and a serenata, and made the acquaintance of the most distinguished Italian musicians, among them, Domenico Scarlatti. These men received him with the greatest cordiality, and expressed the highest admiration both of his compositions, and of his skill as an organist and harpsichordist. In 1709 he returned to Germany, and accepted a conductor's post from the Elector of Hanover, on condition of being allowed to visit England. He accordingly went to London in 1710, and at once composed the opera "*Rinaldo*," to an Italian libretto, for the Haymarket Theater. The work, though written in only fourteen days, was received with the greatest enthusiasm, and Haendel immediately found himself famous. He stayed in London only six months, as his leave of absence had expired, but after his London triumph, his life and work in Hanover no longer contented him.

Early in 1712, he again obtained leave of absence, and coming to London, he lingered far beyond the time allowed him. This naturally offended his master, the elector, and when that prince came to England as George I, Haendel thought it best to avoid showing himself to the new monarch. However, it was soon made up between them. The king arranged some festivity on the Thames, and one of his suite advised Haendel to compose some music for the occasion. This he did, and following the king's barge, in a boat, with his band, he played it, greatly to his majesty's satisfaction. George I was too good a judge of music to deprive himself longer of the services of such a musician, so he not only received him into favor, but granted him an annuity of two hundred pounds.

The two years from 1716 to 1718 Haendel spent with the king in Hanover. Then returning to England, he became chapel-master to the Duke of Chandos, a wealthy nobleman, who lived in a style of great splendor. He remained in this post three years, writing music for the English church service, and harpsichord music for the daughters of the Prince of Wales, who were his pupils. He also wrote here his so-called "Serenata," "*Acis and Galatea*," and "*Esther*," his first English oratorio. He had written a German oratorio, the "*Passion,*" during his last stay in Hanover.

In 1720 he became director of Italian Opera for the Academy of Music, and from this time, for seventeen years, he was constantly engaged in composing operas, and managing operatic enterprises, with varying success. At last, in 1737, he became bankrupt. He made a few ineffectual efforts to recover himself, during the next two years, and then turned his attention almost exclusively to the composition of English oratorios. Here he found his real field. He had had more than forty years of experience as a composer, and all the resources of musical expression then known were perfectly at his command. His imagination was vivid and powerful and dealt, most vigorously with the sublimest religious conceptions. So that in "The Messiah," "Samson," "Saul," "Judas Maccabaeus," and "Israel in Egypt," he created imperishable works, of the loftiest character.

Haendel was a large, vigorous man, open-hearted and generous, passionate and hot-tempered, but very placable, of unconquerable will, energetic, industrious, and withal full of genuine religious feeling. The themes he loved to treat were such as called forth joyful adoration and worship. The two great climaxes in "The Messiah," the "Hallelujah" chorus and "Worthy is The Lamb," are unsurpassed and unsurpassable as expressions of this phase of religious emotion. He could treat the tender and pa-

CHAP. II.

Contrasted with Bach's Passion Music.

thetic aspects of the Messiah's life and work with no less depth and nobility of feeling. Witness his "Behold the Lamb of God," and "He was Despised." A comparison of these with parallel passages in Bach's "Passion Music" will reveal the characteristic differences in the emotional natures of the two men. Bach naturally dwells on the scenes of the Passion and Crucifixion; he dissolves in tears and grief, he melts in contrition, in penitence, in loving, grateful, humble worship. Haendel, too, feels all this, but in a different way, and he does not linger on it; he hastens on to exult in the glorious triumph of the risen Redeemer, to shout forth Hallelujahs in some of the sublimest strains ever uttered by man.

In these oratorios Haendel left his noblest legacy to the world. His organ and harpsichord music, on account of which latter he is necessarily mentioned in this history, was much less significant. Nevertheless, some of it is of permanent value, as, for instance, his "Fire" fugue, and his so-called "Harmonious Blacksmith," and he can not be passed over without honorable mention, since he was, next to Bach, the greatest German organist and harpsichordist of his time, as well as one of the greatest composers of all time. He lived unmarried, died in London April 14, 1759, and was buried in Westminster Abbey.

Domenico Scarlatti.

DOMENICO SCARLATTI, born in Naples in 1683, was the son of ALESSANDRO SCARLATTI, a composer of church music of no small importance in musical history. Domenico's significance lies chiefly in the fact that he was a most brilliant virtuoso upon the harpsichord, and a composer of pieces which not only surprise even the advanced pianists of the present day by their brilliancy and difficulty (they are, in fact, more difficult to play on a modern concert pianoforte than on a harpsichord of Scarlatti's time), but which are of no small musical significance and value. He traveled much, met Haendel in Venice, was some years chapel master at the Vatican, in Rome, played in London, in Lisbon, in Italy again, and finally settled in Madrid, in 1739. Here he remained, admired and respected, as composer and virtuoso, until his death, in 1757.

Scarlatti was not, like Bach and Haendel, a great creative genius of the first rank, but his harpsichord compositions, although greatly inferior in intrinsic significance and permanent influence and value to those of Bach, are probably nearly equal to most of Haendel's, and are even more difficult of execution than any of his, so that in any history of pianoforte music, he must occupy a prominent and an honorable place.

His music compared with Bach and Haendel.

PART SECOND.

THE SECOND CLASSICAL PERIOD.

A. THE EPOCH OF THE DEVELOPMENT OF THE SONATA-FORM.

1750–1800.

CHAPTER III.

MONOPHONIC MUSIC—ITS FORMAL CONSTRUCTION— THE SONATA-FORM.

Monophonic as distinguished from polyphonic music has already been defined. (See Chap. I.) It was originally vocal. The monophonic compositions for the harpsichord grew out of the use of this instrument as an accompaniment to the recitatives and airs of the opera, a form of composition which came into existence in Italy in the latter part of the 16th century.

Chap. III. Monophonic music at first vocal.

These airs and their accompaniments were soon played on the keyed instruments in use, and gradually separate instrumental compositions in the same style came into vogue. These existed side by side with compositions of the prevalent polyphonic style, and gradually became popular. Indeed, the tendency toward the monophonic style showed itself even in many polyphonic compositions for the harpsichord, by such masters as Sebastian Bach and Haendel. In many of their suites, we find, in dances which are essentially polyphonic, numerous instances of sudden chords, filled up to double the number of voice parts properly belonging to the plan. These are hints of the employment of chords in masses, to produce climaxes, or to reinforce loud passages, which is one of the important

Monophonic tendencies in polyphonic music.

characteristics of monophonic music. Many of these dances were also monophonic, in the sense that they had one predominant lyric melody, to which the remaining contrapuntal voices were subordinate.

Scarlatti's Sonatas monophonic.

Domenico Scarlatti went farther, and composed sonatas, monophonic in almost the same sense in which the sonatas of Haydn and Mozart are monophonic. In these, as a rule, only one melody is heard at a time. The accompaniment is made up of chords, more or less full, or of arpeggios. The melody is taken up, now by one voice and now by another, the accompaniment being also transposed.

These sonatas of Scarlatti's are the most eminent examples, known to the present writer, of monophonic music before the death of Sebastian Bach. They are compositions in *one* movement only. The only compositions for the harpsichord in more than one movement, at that time, were the *suites*, previously referred to, partitas and concertos. Sebastian Bach wrote organ sonatas in three movements, and his son Carl Philip Emanuel wrote similar ones for the harpsichord, of which two movements were commonly in the "sonata-form," on a smaller scale than those of later writers.

The Sonata.

The sonata, as now understood, is a composition made up of a series of pieces, commonly three or four, arranged so as to contrast with each other in movement, and in emotional content. A symphony is simply a sonata written for orchestra, differing from the pianoforte sonata only in being laid out on a larger scale. Trios, quartets, quintets, concertos, etc., are composed on the same plan. They are simply sonatas for several instruments. The separate compositions of which a sonata is made up are called "movements," from the fact that they differ in the rate of speed. The more common order is as follows: The first movement is an *allegro*—a rapid, vigorous, spirited or lively composition, somewhat long and elaborate. The second movement is an *adagio*—slow, deeply tender or sad—or else an *andante*—pensive, tender, perhaps melancholy. The third movement is an *allegretto*, perhaps a stately minuet, or a playful *scherzo*. Both these movements are comparatively short. The last movement is a lively *allegro*, or, perhaps, a fiery, rushing *presto*, generally of considerable length. This order is often varied, but the principles of contrast involved in it must always underlie whatever order of movement may be adopted. But the term "Sonata-Form" in its narrow, technical sense, applies, not to the sonata as a whole, but to the *form* of composition commonly adopted in one, or at most two of the separate movements which make up a sonata, the construction of which must now be explained.

First of all, it is necessary to understand clearly what is meant by "form" in music. "Form" has to do with melody, mainly; with the rhythmical regulation of successions of tones, on a large scale. Melody, in order to be intelligible, or any way satisfactory, must be begun, continued and brought to a close in accordance with some definite plan. The

CHAP. III.

Simple periods.

Sections.

Phrases.

chief requirements of this plan, like those of any work of art, are three, viz.: Unity, Variety and Symmetry.

The simplest form of composition which can give any satisfaction, regarded as a completed whole, is a single Period, the nearest analogue of which is a single couplet. A good example of this is in the church tune, "Onward, Christian Soldier," in "Hymns, Ancient and Modern." Here the period is divided into two sections, to fit the two lines of the couplet, and these two sections are balanced against each other, symmetrically. More commonly the two sections of a simple period are each divided by a *cæsura*, or point of partial repose. Indeed, such a division is plainly to be seen in the tune above cited. Each of the two divisions of each section is then called a phrase. More frequently than otherwise, the third phrase is nearly or quite an exact repetition of the first, and the fourth similarly reminds one of the second, that is, they rhyme with each other, so that such a simple period is closely analogous to the ballad stanza. It is, in fact, the form commonly and necessarily used in setting such stanzas to music. The point of repose at the end of the first section (second phrase) is more marked than those which finish the first and third phrases, but is still only a half stop, or musical semicolon. The last section of course closes the period by a full stop. A good example of this form is the first period of the theme in the A major sonata of Mozart (No. 12, Peters' edition).

Another thing must now be noticed about this period, viz.: that what gives *unity* to it is the repeated employment of a single melodic fragment as a *pattern* or *design*. The melodic idea, or "motive," of the first measure is repeated in the second, but in different pitch. The third measure is less obviously an imitation of the first, but still has nothing incongruous with it. The second and fourth phrases have motives differing slightly from that of the first and third, but still analogous to it, and possibly derived from it, or at least suggested by it. This use of one or a few simple motives, of which the case cited is a very simple example, is carried out on the most elaborate scale in all large compositions. In the hands of a master, this multifarious transformation of the original motive invented, prevents unity from becoming uniformity, continually presents them in new and interesting lights, and develops from them, as from germs, a complex and elaborate whole, satfactory to the intellect and to the artistic sense.

When the composer comes to add a second period to his first, this new period will most naturally be a simple one, like the first, made up of two symmetrical sections, balanced against each other as antecedent and consequent. This period, however, must not be wholly new, else we should have not one composition, made up of two periods, but two compositions of *one* complete period each, wholly unrelated. The new period must, of course, contain new materials, or at least a fresh treatment of the old ones, otherwise it would be merely a repetition of the first period.

C

CHAP. III.

But with *variety* there must also be *unity*. The common way of uniting a second period with a first to form a composition is to make the first section of the new period new and fresh, while the second section is a more or less exact repetition of the closing section of the first period. This is precisely the plan of the Mozart example just cited, except that the second period, instead of coming to a full stop at the end of the eight measures, which would make it a simple period, is prolonged by the addition of a phrase of two measures, by which a very effective climax is produced, without in the least impairing the impression of symmetry.

Two period groups combined into a larger whole

This form is the germ from which all the musical forms have sprung. It is in two divisions, balanced against each other as are the two sections of a simple period. It may be enlarged by making each division consist of a period-group of two or more simple periods united. But in the shorter forms, when each simple or prolonged period comes to a full stop, the first division is commonly one period only, the second being composed either of one or two periods, with perhaps a coda. With this is contrasted another similar form, often called a "Trio," after which the original form is repeated, for the sake of unity. This is the form in which marches, waltzes, etc., are written. A good example of it is the *andante* of the sonata in C (No. 2, of the Peters edition) by Mozart. All the slow movements, minuets and scherzi of the Mozart and Beethoven sonatas are in this form, so that examples are easily accessible.

Plan of the sonata-form.

The sonata-form is the most elaborate and extended of the forms which have been developed from the elementary plan given above. Like the forms heretofore cited, it has two main divisions. In its most extended form, as developed in the orchestral symphony, each of these divisions is composed of several period-groups, as follows:

DIVISION I.

I. Principal Subject.
II. Transition.
III. Second Subject (in the Key of the Dominant).
IV. Transition.
V. Conclusion (in the Key of the Dominant).
This division is repeated.

DIVISION II.

I. Elaboration, in which the ideas of the first division are turned over, modulated into different keys, presented in new lights, and combined and developed in various ways.
II. Transition.
III. Repetition of the whole of the first main division, the second subject and conclusion being this time in the key of the Tonic.

Abbreviations of this plan.

In the case of pianoforte sonatas, this form is often abbreviated, by making some of the transitions belong to the period-groups of the main ideas, instead of forming separate groups, and by making the elaboration, and, in fact, nearly all the period-groups shorter than in the most elaborate works. It is to be noted also that in this form the periods which are associated in groups no longer end with full stops. These are reserved for the close of groups or even of larger divisions. The periods follow each other in continuous discourse, and are distinguished from one another not so much by the cadences as by the grouping of the ideas.

Form in polyphonic music.

This is the briefest possible outline of Form, as now developed in monophonic music. In the strict polyphonic style of Sebastian Bach, as shown in his fugues, the most important productions of that style, Form consisted in the orderly arrangement and succession of the different groups formed by the separate entries of the subject and answer. Thus the "exposition" formed the first group, the second complete entry of the subject and answer made a second group, in which the voices entered in a different order, by way of contrast. The same principles of Unity, Variety and Symmetry which underlie the construction of a modern sonata, controlled the fugue also. But there were no "periods," in the monophonic sense. But in Bach's compositions in the free style, as, for instance, in the Gavotte in D minor, in the Sixth English Suite, and in others, we find examples of simple period structure. Indeed, both this gavotte, and the "musette," which alternates with it, are almost exactly in the form of

Simple periods in Bach's dances.

the *andante* of the Mozart sonata in C, cited above. They are polyphonic in the sense that each has more than one real melody; for the bass is a "counterpoint," and not a mere foundation nor a series of accompanying arpeggios. But their form is precisely that of monophonic music, and it is so because there is *one principal melody* to which the counterpoint is subordinate. This melody is necessarily governed by the principles summarized in the above outline, for it is its accordance with these principles that makes it clearly intelligible.

CHAPTER IV.

THE THREE COMPOSERS, THROUGH WHOM THE SONATA-FORM WAS DEVELOPED TO ITS LOGICAL LIMITS:

C. P. E. BACH, 1714–1788.
JOSEPH HAYDN, 1732–1809.
W. A. MOZART, 1756–1791.

CHAP. IV.
C. P. E. Bach.

I. CARL PHILIPP EMANUEL BACH was the third son of Johann Sebastian, and was born at Weimar, March 14, 1714. He was precocious, showed unusual intellectual ability, and though his father taught him music, as a matter of course, he nevertheless planned for him a very different career from that of a musician. He sent him to the Thomas School in Leipzig, and afterwards to the university of the same city, and still later to that at Frankfort-on-the-Oder, to study law. Emanuel thus became a highly educated and cultivated man, and when, in 1737, he determined to relinquish the law for music, he was not only an excellent musician, but a man of such breadth and universality of culture as ensured him a wide influence among men not especially connected with his chosen profession.

His education.

Settles in Berlin at the court of Frederick the Great.

He began his career as a professional musician in Berlin, where he became a great favorite with Frederick the Great. That monarch gave him a special court appointment as chamber-musician and harpsichordist, and being an amateur flute player, he made it Bach's special duty to accompany his solos at his private concerts. Bach held this post until the Seven Years War broke out, in 1757, when he went to Hamburg, became an organist and church music director, and remained there, as musician and composer, until his death in 1788. He wrote large quantities of harpsichord music, some of it with orchestral accompaniment, church music, orchestral music, oratorios, songs, etc., and an important instruction book, "On the true manner of playing the clavichord," which contained his own and the best of his father's ideas on technic, style and interpretation.

Chap. IV.

Removes to Hamburg.

Personally he was kind and polite, and he was always beloved and respected for his personal character, his industry, his ability and attainments as critic, teacher, composer and conductor. His special significance as composer in the history of pianoforte music, lies in the fact, that in his works the decisive step from the polyphonic to the monophonic style was taken.

His place in the History of Music.

In Sebastian Bach, the Fugue had reached its climax. No advance was possible, either in the development of the polyphonic forms, or in their adaptation to the expression of a new content. Progress was now to be made in a wholly new direction. The germs of the monophonic style had existed for more than a century, and this style had even been considerably developed. Short forms

CHAP. IV.
The inevitable course of musical development.

had been developed, more or less unconsciously, "Sonatas" had been written, and enough had already been done, so that, as soon as it had clearly become impossible to do anything more, in the strict polyphonic style, than imitate Sebastian Bach, the channel into which the musical impulse was now to be turned became perfectly clear. The monophonic style was to be cultivated, and to become predominant, and, first of all, the *form* of it was to be developed, the principles of orderly succession of melodic members were to be discovered and established; the means of securing Unity, of enhancing interest by means of Variety and Contrast, and of satisfying the sense of order, symmetry and proportion, were to become familiar by gradual experience, by theory and practice.

Bach's qualifications for leadership in the new movement.

Natural constitution, acquired culture and surrounding circumstances combined to make Emanuel Bach a leader in this new direction. He was not a genius of the highest rank. There was nothing gigantic or colossal about his aims, his ideas, his imagination, his intellectual powers, his emotional capacities or his religious experiences. The reign of the giants had closed with Sebastian Bach and Haendel. To them were to succeed a race of more commonplace musicians, who had, nevertheless, their own special and important work to do.

Emanuel Bach was simply a highly cultivated man, of respectable abilities, a well-trained and accomplished musician, who sought to compose and play in a tasteful, elegant and pleasing style. There seems to have been a sudden reaction in the public mind, against the style of music which Sebastian Bach cultivated, and of which he was the most distinguished representative. After his death, his works fell into speedy oblivion. For almost a century they slumbered, before the world again began to realize what a mighty genius had worked in the old Leipzig cantor, and to seek diligently for the treasures he had left behind, a precious bequest to posterity.

Public taste at that period.

The public seemed tired of the severity of the fugal style; they shunned the bracing intellectual exertion needed for its intelligent comprehension, and preferred music which should give immediate pleasure, without requiring much mental strain on the part of the hearer. Thus it naturally happened that the popular musicians of this generation cultivated the simpler forms of the monophonic style. Into this they imported such ideas of thematic treatment as they could transfer from the older schools of free polyphony. They made it the medium of such expression as they were capable of, and developed and enlarged the small forms according to their intellectual ability. But above all, *taste, elegance*, were the watchwords.

Free polyphony contributes to the monophonic technic.

Emanuel Bach's most important work was in the form he gave the sonata. The sonatas of Scarlatti had been in one movement only, and though this movement was not yet a " Sonata-Form," or " First-movement " form, in the modern sense, it was the germ of it. Its plan was, in general, as follows: It was in two divisions. Division I contained the "exposition" of the sonata. It consisted of several groups of phrases, which perhaps ought to be called periods, since they were commonly separated by more or less decisive cadences, and were generally characterized by different motives. The leading motive of the first period was commonly the most important, being, in fact, a principal subject, all other motives being subordinate and accessory. After this subject had been announced, in the principal key, new motives were introduced, and modulation began, pointing toward a new key in which the division was to close. This key was generally that of the Dominant, if the principal key was major, or if it was minor, then the new key was commonly that of the Relative Major, or sometimes the minor key of the Dominant.

The periods succeeding the first were simply a series of modulatory phrases, often spun out to considerable length, and digressing into a considerable number of more or less closely related keys, before the goal was finally reached. The division was then brought to a close by an extended cadence. There are but very few cases where one of the subordinate motives stands in such a relation to the principal one, and to the others, that it can be fairly called a Second Subject. There is an example of this in No. 7 of Kohler's selections from Scarlatti's sonatas (12 Fugues and Sonatas, Section 3 of the Classical High School for pianists, published by Julius Schuberth & Co., Leipzig). This second subject is lyric, very well contrasted with the principal subject, and the form of the sonata approximates that of Emanuel Bach. But this is an exceptional case, and seems to be the result of accident rather than of design. Still, it shows the direction in which the form of monophonic music was tending.

The second division of the Scarlatti sonata commonly had a plan closely analogous to that of the first division. It started with the principal subject, in the key in which the first division closed, or in some other key not too remote from the original tonic, then introduced the subordinate motives in much the same order as they occurred in the first division, and modulated back to the principal key, in which the sonata began, closing in this key, with an extended cadence. The style of these sonatas was commonly partly monophonic and partly free polyphony. The periods, if periods they must be called, seldom had any definite symmetrical balance of antecedent and consequent. They were irregular as to the number of measures or of phrases, and the composer's sense of symmetry and proportion, though evidently present, seems to have been undeveloped, and to be working blindly, groping its way toward a clearness of form which was not yet attainable.

In these respects, Scarlatti's sonatas were closely analogous to many of the larger dance forms in the suites of his contemporaries, Bach and Haendel. Indeed, the forms of these dances are not distinguishable from that of the so-called "sonatas" in

Division second.

The style of Scarlatti's sonatas.

44 HISTORY OF PIANOFORTE MUSIC.

CHAP. IV.

Symmetry of the smaller dance-forms.

question, and Dr. Hans von Buelow, in his selection of eighteen pieces by Scarlatti (No. 277 of the edition of C. F. Peters, in Leipzig), has given the names of dances of the period to a number of these "sonatas" (with entire propriety, so far as the form and character of the pieces are concerned), for the purpose of making them more attractive. In these writers there are many *small* dance forms which are as regular and symmetrical in the construction and balance of their periods as any to be found in the works of Haydn or Mozart. This was due, probably, to their being founded on *vocal* forms fitted to the ballad stanza, which served as the germ for the development of the monophonic forms. But these larger forms were still more influenced by the elaborate style of the free polyphonic forms, such as the prelude and toccata, than by that of the smaller lyric forms, and partook of the indefiniteness of that style. The lyric and symmetrically formal element was slowly pushing forward into prominence, but had not yet given signs of becoming predominant.

E. Bach's Sonata-Forms.

Emanuel Bach's "Sonata-Forms," which he used in the first and last movements of his sonatas, were very much on the same plan as those of Scarlatti, and of many of the pieces in the suites of Sebastian Bach and Haendel. But his periods are often much more symmetrical than any of those to be found in the previous works alluded to, and there is a much more marked balance of antecedent and consequent. They constitute a distinct advance in clearness of perception of the requirements of Form. They seldom or never contain a well-marked second subject, and the only further advance is in the point that their style is most decidedly monophonic. Imitation there is, and thematic treatment, but the free polyphony or mixed style which had prevailed in the preceding generation in almost all but the smallest and simplest forms, had now given place to a style as decidedly and purely monophonic as that of a Mozart Sonata.

They are decidedly monophonic.

Besides this, Emanuel Bach wrote sonatas in three movements, of which the first and third were "sonata-forms," and the middle one was a lyric slow movement, contrasted with the others in key and in character. This form was adopted from him by Haydn and Mozart, and their sonatas differ from his only in the greater development of the separate movements.

Let us now recapitulate. The modern sonata has four essential characteristics:

Recapitulation.

1. It has at least three movements.
2. These movements are contrasted with one another, in key and in character, some being rapid and lively, others slow and tender.
3. One, at least, of these movements is a "sonata-form."
4. The movements are all monophonic, some predominantly thematic and some lyric.

Of these characteristic features, none were wholly new in Emanuel Bach's time.

Sebastian Bach had written suites in six or seven

movements; but these were all *in the same key.* Moreover, some of them were in free polyphony. His Partitas were simply small suites. He wrote "Sonatas" for the organ in three movements, the first and third being *allegros* and the middle one an *adagio* or an *andante,* but these were all strictly polyphonic. He also wrote sonatas for the harpsichord, but these differed from his suites only in admitting fugues and other forms which were not dance-forms. Finally, he had written concertos in three movements, the first and last being allegros and the middle one an *andante* or *adagio,* in a style as closely approaching monophony as did the sonatas of Scarlatti. These probably served Emanuel Bach as models for his sonatas. But the three movements of these concertos were all in the same key.

Haendel had written suites which resembled the sonatas of Bach. They had sometimes fewer, sometimes more movements. Of these, one was often a fugue. They were generally all in the same key.

Of Scarlatti's sonatas, enough has been said.

It will be seen that no one characteristic feature of the sonata was original with Emanuel Bach, nor did he even develop the "Sonata-Form" much further than his predecessors. What he did do that had not been done before was this: He combined *all* the essential characteristics of the sonata in numerous compositions of such merit that they became models for his contemporaries and his immediate successors. He brought the exclusively monophonic sonata into vogue; he contributed toward its development in the direction of clearness and symmetry; he adopted the principle of contrast in key as well as in character, in the three movements of which his sonatas were composed; in short, he established the plan of the sonata, determined the direction in which it was to develop, and, by his influence and example, gave the most powerful impulse to that development.

II. FRANZ (*English*, FRANCIS,) JOSEPH HAYDN was born April 1, 1732, in the little Austrian village of Rohrau. His father was a wheelwright. His mother, before her marriage, was a cook in a noble family. They were honest, industrious, pious people, fond of music, but wholly untrained in it. Little Joseph used to sing with them their simple songs, in a beautiful, clear, childish soprano. His father saw in him evidences of musical talent, and as there was no opportunity for his proper training at home, he was removed to school at Hainburg, some four leagues from home, at the early age of six. Here a relative of his, named Frankh, became his teacher. The boy was thoroughly well taught, proved an apt pupil, and learned to sing well and to play different instruments.

At the age of eight, Reutter, court-composer and conductor at St. Stephen's church, Vienna, being at Hainburg on a visit, heard him sing, and at once offered him a place in his choir. So the boy went to Vienna, sang in the cathedral choir, continued his musical studies, and also those of the school curriculum. His music lessons did not include in-

F.J.Haydn.

His early schooling.

Goes to Vienna as choir singer.

struction in Harmony or Composition, but so strong was his natural bent in this direction that he constantly practiced it by himself, working hard and spoiling vast quantities of music-paper. Five years after he went to Vienna, his voice began to change, and being of no further use as a singer, he was soon dismissed to shift for himself. He struggled on, amidst poverty and hardship, practiced the violin and harpsichord, gave lessons for his daily bread, and assiduously devoted himself to the study and practice of composition.

He soon made the acquaintance of some of Emanuel Bach's sonatas, was greatly interested in them, and thenceforth they became his models. Bach afterwards declared that Haydn alone thoroughly understood his style. He procured all the theoretical works he could lay hands on, mastered their contents, and gradually exercised himself in every species of composition. He wrote masses, operas, string-quartets, and, by dint of hard work, speedily attained certainty and facility of technic, and independence and originality of style.

He began to make friends. A wealthy amateur named von Fuernberg invited him to his house, gave him opportunities to hear good performances of chamber music, and encouraged him to write his first string quartet. His lessons increased, and his price was raised. His compositions found sale among wealthy lovers of music. In 1759 he became conductor of a small but good orchestra in the employ of Count Morzin, and wrote his first symphony for it in the same year. There was at that time no musical public. Artists were obliged to depend solely on the patronage of the wealthy. Haydn's salary as conductor was two hundred florins (about one hundred dollars). Of course living was cheap.

Chap. IV.

He determined to marry, and in 1760, Maria Anna Keller, daughter of a wigmaker, who had been his pupil, became his wife. She was three years older than he, had a bad temper, had no sympathy whatever with his aims as an artist, and was every way unsuited to be the companion of such a man. She made his domestic life miserable till their separation, a few years before her death in 1800.

His marriage.

Count Morzin was obliged to dismiss his orchestra soon after this, and in 1761, Haydn entered the service of Prince Esterhazy, at Eisenstadt, his country seat in Hungary, as conductor of an orchestra of only sixteen members. But they were good players, and he was at once stimulated to do his best in composing for them. This orchestra had a chorus and solo singers associated with it for service in church and at concerts, and Werner, Haydn's predecessor, now an old man, remained for a time in charge of the church music. The orchestra was gradually increased, concerts were frequent, rehearsals were required daily, and Haydn had enough to do, with conducting and providing new compositions. Here he remained for nearly thirty years, and composed a vast amount of music, symphonies,

Is made conductor to Prince Esterhazy.

Vast number of his works.

chamber music, harpsichord and pianoforte music, church music, songs, operettas, etc., until the orchestra was finally disbanded. He then returned to Vienna, but was immediately invited to London, by Salomon, the English publisher. Thither he went, in the winter of 1790–1. Before this, he had become acquainted with Mozart, had formed the highest opinion of his genius, and the two had become warm friends.

Visits London.

In London he was received with the greatest enthusiasm. He composed six symphonies for Salomon's concerts, conducted them at the pianoforte, and afterwards gave other concerts, all of which were extremely successful. He remained about a year and a half, and then returned to Vienna. Early in 1794, he again went to London under a similar engagement, and succeeded even more brilliantly in all respects. He earned fame and money, and returned home in 1795, comfortably independent. He still retained the title of conductor to Prince Esterhazy, and the orchestra was now revived. He continued to compose for it several years. His reputation was greatly increased by his oratorios, "The Creation," first given April 29, 1798, and "The Seasons," composed the following year. This was the last of his important works. He died May 31, 1809.

His two oratorios.

Personal characteristics.

Haydn was a small, short man, very dark, with dark gray eyes. In disposition he was cheerful and even tempered, and though he was sensitive, and unhappy in his domestic affairs, his music gives no evidence that his mental equanimity was ever greatly disturbed. He was very devout, very diligent in his work, and commanded universal respect. He composed very carefully and deliberately, attaching the utmost importance to the working out of his themes, aiming always to develop each idea naturally, evolving from it, as from a germ, a work whose prime characteristic should be organic unity. He was indeed precise and careful, but he was no pedantic follower of rules. Whatever sounded well or answered the ends he had in view, he was content to write down, regardless of grammatical rules as laid down by the theorists of his time. He was a genuine creator, and his fund of invention seemed inexhaustible. "The Creation," the child of his old age, equals in freshness of melodic invention any work of his youth or prime, and retains its charm to this day.

As might be expected from his position as leader of an orchestra, and composer for this and for concerts of chamber music, it is in the two departments of the symphony and the string quartet, that his originality exerted the strongest and most far-reaching influence. His numerous compositions in these fields were so superior in form and style to anything that preceded them, that they drove them all into oblivion, became models for succeeding composers, and gained for Haydn the rightful title of "the father of instrumental music." But in the field of pianoforte music his influence was hardly less marked. Accepting the form of the sonata as

Chiefly a composer of orchestral music.

His pianoforte music and its influence.

established by Emanuel Bach, he enlarged all its movements and developed in the "sonata-form" that clear and definite order of period and period-groups which made it strictly and in the fullest sense classical. In his sonata-forms, there is a "first subject," often carried out into a period-group of considerable length, a transition period or period-group, then a "second subject," equally extensive, a transition and a conclusion. The second division begins with an elaboration of the ideas of the first division, followed by a repetition of that division exactly on the plan described in the preceding chapter on Form. The student may examine them for himself in the very cheap but excellent complete edition of his sonatas published by C. F. Peters, in Leipzig; or the selection of ten celebrated sonatas, published by the same house, may serve as characteristic specimens of his form and style.

WOLFGANG AMADEUS MOZART, born at Salzburg, January 27, 1756, was the son of Leopold Mozart, an intelligent, well-educated and every way superior musician, in the service of the Archbishop of Salzburg. He was extremely precocious, began to manifest remarkable love for music when only three years old, soon learned to play the harpsichord and the violin, and even began to compose. He had the most delicate ear, was extremely quick and intelligent, learned by intuition everything pertaining to music, and in short, showed the most unmistakable evidences of possessing the innate gift of genius. Withal he was amiable in disposition, perfectly teachable, tenderly attached to his family and to all who were kind to him, and so profited by all the instruction he received. His sister, Maria Anna, two years older than he, was also very talented, so much so that their father thought it worth while to make concert tours with the two children to exhibit their remarkable gifts to the various noblemen, whose patronage, in those days, was the only support of artists.

Concert tours.

The first of these tours was undertaken when Wolfgang was only six years of age. They went to Munich, and afterwards to Vienna, where Wolfgang's genius excited the liveliest interest and admiration in the Emperor and in all his court. The Empress petted him, and with the frankness of a warm-hearted child, wholly ignorant of distinctions of rank, and of the restraints of court etiquette, he jumped up into her lap, threw his arms around her neck and kissed her, doubtless to the great amusement of the courtiers. The next year they went to Paris, where four of his sonatas for pianoforte and violin were published, and afterward to London, where he was received with the greatest enthusiasm by the king, the royal family, the nobility, the musicians, and the public. His powers of improvisation excited the greatest astonishment and admiration. Musicians delighted to put him to the severest tests, from which he invariably came off triumphant. In 1765 they started for home, giving concerts by the way in Holland, Paris, Switzerland, and various German cities.

His unembarrassed treatment of royalty.

CHAP. I I.

Tour in Italy.

His spontaneity of invention.

After these tours, he continued diligently to study and compose at Salzburg, under his father's direction. He went also to Vienna, and in 1769 his father began with him a tour of the Italian cities, both to enlarge his musical experience, and to extend his reputation. The tour was every way successful. The boy learned much, and his genius was everywhere admired and respected. At Bologna he met the celebrated Padre Martini, who gave him lessons in fugue and strict counterpoint. He composed a good deal in Italy, among other things, an opera, and several symphonies.

After their return to Salzburg, in 1771, study and composition went on with even greater vigor. The boy's invention was exhaustless. Melodies rose in his imagination like water in a boiling spring, and in all that pertained to the development and technical treatment of his ideas, there seemed no limit to his capabilities. He wrote church music, chamber music, symphonies, harpsichord music, operas, all with no apparent effort, and with the utmost rapidity. He was indeed an artist "by the grace of God." These early compositions were, indeed, of little permanent value, but his powers were maturing by exercise, and he was gathering materials and gaining in experience daily. In spite of the universal admiration of his gifts and attainments, his father found it impossible to obtain for him a court appointment. He was, indeed, vice-conductor to the Archbishop of Salzburg, but without a salary, and his relations to his patron were by no means pleasant. So, at the age of twenty-one, he severed this connection, and started with his mother for Paris. But there the time and circumstances proved unfavorable, and soon his mother died there.

He returned to Salzburg, and accepted the place of organist and concert-meister to the court and cathedral. But he found it impossible to live with the Archbishop. The troubles culminated in Vienna, whither Mozart had been summoned in March, 1781, his master being there on a visit. This dignified prelate was very fond of lording it over those in his service. He made his court composer eat with the servants, addressed him in terms of vile abuse, and finally, being displeased with him, for no discoverable reason, ordered him to leave the house. Mozart left, and never had anything to do with him afterward. To the honor of the Emperor, and of the Viennese nobility, be it said that they all hated this detestable despiser of genius, and treated him with contempt.

On the 16th of August, 1782, Mozart married Constanze Weber, third daughter of Fridolin Weber, a prompter and copyist, whose acquaintance Wolfgang had made sometime before, in Mannheim, but who was now living in Vienna. The marriage was a happy one, but Constanze was a poor manager, and Mozart was careless in money matters, so that they were constantly in financial embarrassment from their marriage until Mozart's death. The Emperor and the nobility might very easily have made the life of the great composer an easy one, as regards money matters. Why this was not done is a mystery, since they seemed to appreciate the fact that his was a genius such as is sent into the world but seldom, but certain it is that he was unable to obtain a conductor's appointment, or any other lucrative position. Men greatly his inferior were preferred to him, and he earned a precarious livelihood by giving lessons, playing at concerts, and the sale of his compositions.

His great operas.
Among the most important of his works were his operas, of which he wrote many for Vienna, Prague, and other cities. The greatest of these are "Don Juan," "Figaro's Wedding," and "The Magic Flute;" next to these, "The Abduction from the Seraglio," "Idomeneus," "Titus" and "Cosi fan tutte." He also wrote many symphonies, which were an advance on Haydn's in the extent of their development, and in the greater fullness and richness of their instrumentation. His chamber music also surpassed all that had been written by his predecessors. He wrote with the greatest ease and produced immense quantities of music, but the constant strain, added to his anxieties about money matters and to the drain on his vitality made by the constant excitements of his life, sapped his strength.

Overwork and early death.
He died December 5, 1791, poor and in debt, and was buried in the common pauper's grave, in the churchyard of St. Mary. Thus was sacrificed to the niggardliness of titled fools a man worth more to the world than whole countries full of emperors, counts and dukes.

In figure, Mozart was short and small; he had a prominent nose, and was not remarkable for being either good looking or the reverse. In disposition he was amiable and kind, very vivacious and fond of society, and very fond of his friends, who loved him in return. Between him and Haydn there existed a warm friendship. Mozart always acknowledged his obligations to his older fellow-composer, and spoke of his works with great admiration and respect. On his part, Haydn cordially recognized Mozart's genius. In 1785, on hearing some of Mozart's quartets, he said to Leopold Mozart, "I declare to you before God, as a man of honor, that your son is the greatest composer that I know, either personally or by reputation; he has taste, and beyond that the most consummate knowledge of the art of composition."

As a composer, Mozart was remarkable, first of all for spontaneity and fertility of invention, and next, perhaps, for sensuous beauty of melody and harmony and warmth of color in modulation and instrumentation. In his best operas he also achieved much in the way of truthful dramatic characterization. In his pianoforte sonatas and concertos, which more immediately concern us in this history, he made decided advances on Haydn in the development of Form. His greatest compositions in this kind were laid out on a broader scale than any of Haydn's; they were perfect in Unity, and admirable in Symmetry and Proportion. They were not remarkable for strong contrasts, but contrast is not of gards money matters. Why this was not done is a mystery, since they seemed to appreciate the fact that his was a genius such as is sent into the world but seldom, but certain it is that he was unable to obtain a conductor's appointment, or any other lucrative position. Men greatly his inferior were preferred to him, and he earned a precarious livelihood by giving lessons, playing at concerts, and the sale of his compositions.

His great operas.

Among the most important of his works were his operas, of which he wrote many for Vienna, Prague, and other cities. The greatest of these are "Don Juan," "Figaro's Wedding," and "The Magic Flute;" next to these, "The Abduction from the Seraglio," "Idomeneus," "Titus" and "Cosi fan tutte." He also wrote many symphonies, which were an advance on Haydn's in the extent of their development, and in the greater fullness and richness of their instrumentation. His chamber music also surpassed all that had been written by his predecessors. He wrote with the greatest ease and produced immense quantities of music, but the constant strain, added to his anxieties about money matters and to the drain on his vitality made by the constant excitements of his life, sapped his strength.

Overwork and early death.

He died December 5, 1791, poor and in debt, and was buried in the common pauper's grave, in the churchyard of St. Mary. Thus was sacrificed to the niggardliness of titled fools a man worth more to the world than whole countries full of emperors, counts and dukes.

In figure, Mozart was short and small; he had a prominent nose, and was not remarkable for being either good looking or the reverse. In disposition he was amiable and kind, very vivacious and fond of society, and very fond of his friends, who loved him in return. Between him and Haydn there existed a warm friendship. Mozart always acknowledged his obligations to his older fellow-composer, and spoke of his works with great admiration and respect. On his part, Haydn cordially recognized Mozart's genius. In 1785, on hearing some of Mozart's quartets, he said to Leopold Mozart, "I declare to you before God, as a man of honor, that your son is the greatest composer that I know, either personally or by reputation; he has taste, and beyond that the most consummate knowledge of the art of composition."

Mozart's personal appearance and character.

Haydn's estimate of him.

As a composer, Mozart was remarkable, first of all for spontaneity and fertility of invention, and next, perhaps, for sensuous beauty of melody and harmony and warmth of color in modulation and instrumentation. In his best operas he also achieved much in the way of truthful dramatic characterization. In his pianoforte sonatas and concertos, which more immediately concern us in this history, he made decided advances on Haydn in the development of Form. His greatest compositions in this kind were laid out on a broader scale than any of Haydn's; they were perfect in Unity, and admirable in Symmetry and Proportion. They were not remarkable for strong contrasts, but contrast is not of

The characteristics of his style.

CHAP. IV.
Repose, not contrast, an essential element of the classical.

the essential nature of the classical. Variety there was, an inexhaustible freshness of ideas and of treatment, and repose, which is of the very essence of the strictly classical, of which he and Haydn were the foremost representatives. With Mozart, the Sonata, considered as an Art-Form, reached its culmination. He had developed it to its logical limits, and thenceforth little or no advance was to be made upon his work, so far as form was concerned. The great composers who immediately succeeded him adopted his forms at first. They afterward struck out new paths for themselves, but the new development was not in the direction of elaborate forms, but of a new content, and of the adaptation of forms to the embodiment of this content. This will be treated of in the next epoch.

The student is advised to compare the forms of the pianoforte works of Emanuel Bach, Haydn and Mozart, for himself. The complete sonatas and concertos of Mozart may be obtained very cheaply in the Peters' edition.

CHAPTER V.

The Epoch of the Predominance of Content in the Sonata.

THE CONTENT OF MUSIC.

The content of a musical composition is what is contained in it;—the ideas and feelings which find expression through it, and the ideals which are embodied in it.

Chap. V. Content defined.

1. What ideas, then, may be expressed in the forms of music? 2. What feelings, if any? 3. What ideals may be embodied in it?

1. No images can be expressed or conveyed by combinations or successions of tones. No events can be described in this way, no situations indicated, except indirectly and with difficulty. Nor can any abstract ideas be expressed. Certain sounds do indeed suggest certain ideas and images, and may be employed in music for this purpose. Thus the barking of a dog raises the idea of the animal, because we have always associated the sound with dogs, but the idea of a dog given by this sound alone is extremely incomplete, so that any one confined to a mere imitation of barking in an attempt to express and convey his idea of any particular dog, would be very unsuccessful. Given other par-

Music can not express images or abstract ideas.

CHAP. V.

Suggestions of ideas by music must always be incidental.

ticulars, and the mere suggestion by this sound would be sufficient to raise the complete idea.

There are instances of this kind in music. Thus, Mendelssohn in his music to Shakespeare's Midsummer Night's Dream, introduces in the midst of music appropriate to a love scene, an imitation of the braying of a donkey, and this irresistibly suggests at once the scene with *Bottom* and *Titania*, which Mendelssohn had in mind. But if we did not know beforehand that the composer's music referred to this particular play, the mere introduction of a bray would convey no such idea.

We must discard then, at the outset, any notion that music can be used as words are, or as the pictorial arts are, for the expression and conveyance of the images impressed on our minds by outward objects. Any use of music for such a purpose must be incidental and secondary to its main object. There has been a great deal of nonsense written about "the meaning of music," by writers who wished to connect some definite scene or event with particular pieces, importing into them a significance wholly foreign to the composer's intention.

All talk about "describing" this or that event or situation in tones indicates confusion of thought. Properly speaking, no music ever "described" or "depicted" anything. The expressions used, however, are attempts to convey a real truth, the relations of which are apparently not clear in the minds of the writers who use them. More of this hereafter.

But are there, then, no *ideas* in music? Certainly there are; but *only musical ideas*, except, as in the above illustrations, when other ideas are indirectly suggested.

<small>What musical ideas are.</small>

What, then, is a *musical idea?* A musical idea is any succession or combination of musical sounds, the separate components of which have a definite, intelligible relation to one another. " Motives," as defined in Chapter III, are musical ideas. The development, arrangement and combination of these motives, so as to evolve from them complex wholes, satisfactory to the intellect, constitutes *musical thought*.

<small>Musical thought defined.</small>

The proper apprehension of the completed product of the composer's thought, as coherent, logical musical discourse, is also to be called musical thinking. A fugue, sonata or symphony, studied scientifically, in all the relations of the separate parts to one another and to the whole, demands for its proper comprehension intellectual powers and training. Considered from the side of construction, of technical knowledge and technical treatment of sounds, music is purely a product of intellect and the composition of it is a purely intellectual process.

But no composer of genius impresses himself on the world merely or mainly as an intellectual athlete, or as a *skillful* composer. His skill is subordinate, —is only a means to an end. That end is the embodiment of some ideal. Mere technical skill, dexterity in the combination and arrangement of sounds may be acquired by diligent study. It may

<small>Technical attainments are means to an end.</small>

be possessed as an attainment by scholars and pedants without a spark of creative power. But the real creative artist uses the materials accumulated by study, and the facility acquired by practice, as so much food for his imagination; as means for the embodiment of ideal conceptions. First and foremost, that which occupies the attention of the artist is the embodiment of ideals of *Beauty*. It is not enough that his production be skillfully constructed; it must be *beautiful* in order to satisfy his artistic sense and make for itself a permanent place in the world's estimation.

Beauty in music.

Beauty in music is of three kinds: Sensuous Beauty of Tone, Symmetrical Beauty of Form, and the Beauty which comes of the adequate expression of a worthy emotional content. Of these three kinds of Beauty, any one may predominate, almost to the exclusion of the other two; or two of them may be prominently present, the other being neglected; or all three may unite to form a well-rounded and satisfactory whole.

Of these three kinds, compositions which embody simply an ideal of the Pleasing in Sensation, are lowest in the scale, because the production of them involves the minimum of intellectual effort and of technical attainment, and also because the emotional content is inferior. Compositions which combine with this the embodiment of an ideal of Formal Beauty stand higher, because Form is the result of high intellectual processes.

Before passing to the consideration of music as

the expression of ideal emotional experiences, it is extremely important to make sure that there is no confusion in the minds of even young readers, unacquainted with psychology, as to the relation of feeling to the other mental operations; and also that the distinctions between the different kinds of feelings are clearly understood. The discussion of this subject, even in the briefest possible way, involves a long digression, for which, it is hoped, ample excuse will be found in the importance of the the subject, the widespread ignorance of it, and the difficulty of referring students to any treatise on it which shall be at once brief, clear and pointed. No one can really understand music, who can not discriminate between its emotional content and the other elements which enter into it. It is hoped, therefore, that sufficient apology has already been offered for the interpolation of a short essay on the emotions here.

Importance of a clear idea of feeling.

There are three, and only three kinds of activity possible to the human mind. We know, we feel, we choose. There are three general faculties corresponding to these mental activities, viz.: the Intellect, the Sensibility and the Will.

Different kinds of mental activity.

Under the intellect are included all perceptions, Memory, Imagination, logical Thinking, Intuition, in short all cognition or knowing. The will is the power of choosing. Under the sensibility are included all those phenomena of mind which we commonly speak of as Feeling or Emotion, these terms being here used as synonymous, from the simplest

CHAP. V.

Simple emotions.

experiences of pleasure and pain to the warmest affections, the strongest desires and the most violent passions.

Feelings are either (1) simple, or (2) complex.

I. The simple emotions are pure feelings of pleasure or pain. They are in all cases effects, produced upon the mind by a great variety of causes. The attempt to classify and enumerate these causes would lead us too far. It is sufficient to note that the mind is always affected by some cause or other which produces either pleasure or pain, although our emotions are sometimes so lacking in intensity that the sensibility seems to be almost neutral;—the line of transition from one state to the other is nearly reached, and feeling is reduced to a minimum for the time being. This is especially true when there is no cause at work which powerfully affects the feelings, and when the mind is taken up with intellectual operations. A man absorbed in solving a mathematical problem, or in composing a fugue or sonata, for example, may be so occupied with his purely intellectual activity that he is almost or quite unconscious of feeling at all. Nevertheless, there is feeling present. For if his intellectual energy is put forth without impediment, the exercise of his intellectual powers is pleasurable; if he meets with unexpected obstacles or interruptions, a painful effect is produced. The pain in the one case or the pleasure in the other may be of considerable intensity, or it may be so slight as not to obtrude itself on the attention, and the state of feeling, or mood, besides being simple, may be said to be indefinite or vague.

The simple emotions of pleasure and pain often depend on bodily conditions as causes, without our being conscious of what these causes are. Most people are subject to elations and depressions of mood, dependent on the condition of the nervous system. The nerves may be affected by the weather, by the condition of the digestive apparatus, or by other bodily causes. Besides this we receive pleasure and pain from our social relations, from success or failure in our business, from the gratifications or thwarting of desire, etc., etc.

Often depend upon bodily conditions.

II. Complex feelings are either (1) Desires or (2) Affections. (Passions are simply desires in their extreme form.) 1. When we experience pleasure in view of some object as an exciting cause, we commonly *desire* that object in its absence; or if any object gives us pain, we desire its absence. In both cases there is something more than a simple emotion. There is superadded to the pure pleasure or pain an *outgoing* of the mind toward the cause of the feeling to possess it, or to be rid of it. The mind is no longer simply *passive*, quiescent; it reaches out actively toward its object. Desire tends to action. Thus we enjoy a beautiful object, or the society of a friend. The withdrawal of these causes a painful sense of lack and deprivation; we desire a renewal of the pleasure before experienced, and long for the presence of the friend or the beautiful object as a condition of the wished-for gratification.

Complex feelings.

Desire tends to action.

CHAP. V.

In the case of a friend, we desire not only his presence but his society, interchange of thought and feeling; we desire also that our thoughts, feelings and actions may meet the approval of those we esteem. In the case of a beautiful object, or any object which gives us pleasure, we desire to possess it, to have it within our control; or if that be impossible, as in the case of a landscape, for instance, we desire to appropriate it, to make it our own so far as the nature of the case admits. Or, we are repelled by something ugly or horrible, or displeased by behavior which we disapprove; we desire to separate ourselves from the disagreeable person or object, and this feeling tends to active effort on our part to bring about this separation.

The affections.

2. Affections involve still another mode of feeling. We experience pleasure or pain; we recognize some person or sentient being as the cause of this simple emotion; there is a movement of feeling to confer good or ill upon the cause. With this is also commonly associated the desire of possession. The society of a friend delights us. We not only desire the presence, society and approbation of our friend, but we desire also that he should experience pleasure. This awakens in us the impulse to please him, to act for his good. Or we are displeased by the behavior of an evil-disposed person. We not only desire the absence of so obnoxious a cause of painful emotion, but we are naturally impelled to inflict pain on the offender.

The important consideration for us in this discussion, as regards the content of music, is, that in the simple emotions the mind is passive and quiescent; in the complex experiences of the desires and affections there is a strong tendency to action. These are the impulses which furnish motive power to the will, and are the springs of conduct and of character.

The significance of these distinctions will appear more and more clearly as we attempt to study the works of various composers, and to interpret their mental states from their productions. We shall find that some of these compositions give evidences that their authors were occupied primarily with the intellectual side of their work,—with plans of construction. In these cases emotional experience was reduced to a simple mood, so vague that close scrutiny would be required to decide whether it was pleasurable or painful. We shall find other cases in which the completed products show that the composer had thoroughly mastered his material, constructed his forms with unimpeded freedom of energy and experienced keen pleasure in the spontaneous activity of production. This pleasure became the emotional content of the music without the deliberate intention and perhaps without the consciousness of the composer. In other cases, there was added to this a higher faculty in the composer whereby he conceived an Ideal of Beauty, which he sought to embody in his composition. In these cases there was infused into the work the added delight arising from the contemplation of the beauti-

Relation of these distinctions to our understanding of the content of music.

ful conception, and from the consciousness of success in the attempt to embody it.

In all these cases the emotions experienced by the composer were simple, except in so far as the element of desire to accomplish a certain result complicated his emotional state. When this desire was constantly in process of fulfillment this element was reduced to the smallest possible quantity, and the feeling became as nearly simple as possible.

Some imposers passionate.
But we shall find composers in whose mental states the complex feelings predominated; whose minds are no longer occupied mainly with intellectual processes, but in whom urgent desires, longings and yearnings, or fierce passions constantly force themselves upon consciousness, make their impulses felt in the whole mental activity, and leave unmistakable traces on the completed product. We shall

Some deliberately seek to express emotion.
find others who consciously sought to express in tones real or imagined emotional experiences; who deliberately set themselves the task of finding successions and combinations of tones which should embody clearly conceived emotional states,—sought to reproduce in tones the most subtle as well as the most powerful impressions made upon their own sensibility, and to convey these impressions to others. Finally, we shall find composers who sought to reproduce the emotional impressions made by a series of events, with such vividness, that a single clue should suffice to suggest the whole story to those already acquainted with it.

THE CONTENT OF MUSIC.

Resuming now our discussion of the content of music, let us inquire: *How* are these feelings revealed through musical composition? What is the relation of music to emotion? This is now for us the inquiry of most immediate importance.

Every one who will give the matter a little attention will discover that sounds, articulate and inarticulate, are among the most efficient means of expressing and conveying feelings. Animals express pleasure and pain by means of inarticulate sounds; so do infants. Adults do the same, and modify their expressions of ideas in language by the tones in which their words are uttered. These tones express and convey the emotional state of the speakers. We all learn in early childhood to associate certain modulations of the voices of those around us with certain feelings in their minds, so that we could not possibly be convinced that we do not interpret these sounds correctly. So certain are we of our understanding of them, that no positiveness of assertion by any one as to the state of his feelings could convince us that he spoke truly, if his tone of voice belied his assertion. Thus anger, hatred, joy, love, jealousy, eager expectation, desire, passionate remorse, gentle regret, sadness or melancholy are conveyed unmistakably by sounds, whether connected with words or not. Let it be noticed that *words*, the *signs* of *ideas*, only excite feelings *indirectly*, by conveying ideas, which raise the feelings; while *sounds* convey these feelings *directly* and immediately. It is by the natural extension and carry-

CHAP. V.

The relation of music to emotion.

Sounds express feelings.

Words express ideas.

ing out of this process, that the sounds produced by instruments have come to be associated with the same feelings which the voice expresses by tones in speech and in song, so that music has come to be a highly complex and elaborate *language* of *emotion* — a perfect medium for the expression of feeling.

Music a language of feeling.

This is the prime characteristic of music. All the fine arts aim to express and excite feeling. The painter deals in pictures of stirring or tender or tragic scenes; the poet and the novelist describe and narrate situations and events which excite the strongest and deepest feelings. But, as already pointed out, the office of words is to express *directly, ideas;* the painter gives us still more clearly ideas and images. Feelings are indeed excited by the ideas, but the process by which the artist reaches other minds is a duplex one. The musician reaches the sensibility of his hearers *at once*, and *directly*, without the intervention of images. This is the peculiarity of music among the fine arts, that it expresses the life of emotion most directly, and most subtly and powerfully. That music is greatest and noblest which most perfectly answers this, its peculiar end and aim; in which its peculiar capacity is most fully recognized and developed.

That composer is greatest who most clearly discerns the true ends and capabilities of his art; who aims to give worthy expression to the noblest emotional experience. He is the best connoisseur who best appreciates the capabilities of music as a language of emotion, and is best able to interpret

Who is the best composer and critic?

the emotional state of the composer by hearing his productions.

Chap. V.

It is, therefore, not only possible to embody in music ideals of emotional experience, but the embodiment of such ideals constitutes its peculiar and appropriate function, and all worthy embodiment of noble emotions involves Beauty, as well as do products which attain or approximate ideal perfection of form.

Those compositions then, are greatest and noblest which, using as materials tones pleasing by their sensuous beauty, combine them into symmetrical wholes, satisfactory to the intellect, and express through these combinations emotional experiences ideally noble and exalted.

What compositions are highest in rank.

To sum up this discussion: In a broad sense, the ideals of the Pleasing in Sensation and of Beauty of Form which are embodied in music may be said to be a part of its content, but that which is most appropriately said to be "contained" in music, is the emotional experience which finds expression through the form; this it is which is innermost, and so with peculiar propriety is said to be "The Content of Music." In this sense the term "content" will always be used in this book. Wherever it appears, *emotional content* is meant.*

---

*The reader's attention is called to Herbert Spencer's essay on "The Origin and Function of Music" in his "Illustrations of Universal Progress;" to "Music and Morals," by the Rev. H. R. Haweis; and to "How to Understand Music," by W. S. B. Mathews. These books are invaluable to any student who desires to obtain a clear comprehension of the relation of music to emotion.

CHAPTER VI.

LUDWIG VAN BEETHOVEN.

1770-1827.

THE COMPOSER WHO EMBODIED IN THE SONATA THE NOBLEST POSSIBLE CONTENT, AND RAISED IT TO THE HIGHEST SIGNIFICANCE AS A WORK OF ART.

Chap. VI.

L. van Beethoven.

Birth and family.

LUDWIG VAN BEETHOVEN was born in Bonn, December 16, 1770. His father, Johann, was a tenor singer in the employ of the Elector of Cologne, and was by no means a man of high character, being more or less dissipated in his habits, and rough and harsh in his manners. His mother was daughter of the chief cook at Ehrenbreitstein, and was an easygoing, kind-hearted person. They were very poor, having no income except Johann's salary as singer, which was only three hundred florins, about one hundred and fifty dollars a year. When Ludwig was four years old, his father began to teach him music, giving him lessons on the violin and harpsichord. He also sent him to a common school until he was thirteen years old, where he learned reading, writing, arithmetic, and the rudiments of Latin. This was all the formal schooling he ever had, but he afterwards studied Latin, Italian and French privately with one Zambona, who gave him help and intellectual stimulus in various ways. At the age of nine years he was turned over to another music teacher named Pfeiffer, who gave him efficient instruction for a year, and at the same time he took lessons on the organ of the court organist, Van den Eeden. A year or so later, Van den Eeden was succeeded by Neefe, who then became young Ludwig's teacher, and proved of very great service to him. By the time he was eleven years old, Ludwig was able to take his master's place at the organ in his absence, was an excellent player and sight-reader, and had played nearly all of Bach's "Well-tempered Clavichord."

A little more than a year from this time, Neefe was appointed to be director of both sacred and secular music in Bonn, and young Beethoven, child though he was, was given charge of the harpsichord in the theater orchestra, as accompanist and conductor of the rehearsals. This gave him a great deal of practice and experience, for many good operas were given, but for more than a year it brought him no pay; at the end of that time, he began to receive a salary of one hundred and fifty florins (about seventy-five dollars) per year. He practiced composition, writing songs and pianoforte pieces during this time and gaining in knowledge and experience.

In 1785 he took violin lessons of Franz Ries, and wrote three quartets for pianoforte and strings, besides continuing his composition of smaller pieces, and two years later he paid a visit to Vienna, where

CHAP. VI.
His music teachers.

Violin lessons.

he met Mozart and took a few lessons from him. This was, of course, an important event in the life of the young composer. Mozart recognized his inborn genius, and predicted a great future for him.

Makes valuable friends.

A little later, Beethoven acquired some friends, who were not only of the greatest importance to his development at this critical age (he was now seventeen), but who remained devotedly attached to him during his life. These were the Von Breuning family and Count Waldstein, a young nobleman, eight years older than Ludwig, a cultivated young man, and an intelligent amateur musician. Madame Von Breuning was a refined, intellectual, cultivated widow, with three sons and a daughter. She employed young Ludwig as a music teacher in her family, and they all became his warm friends. Up to this time, his associations had probably been, for the most part, with uncultivated people. His family, as we have seen, was low in station, and far from elevated in character, so that there was nothing in his home surroundings to develop refinement. Indeed, he remained through life a boor in his manners, and was always an uncomfortable person to live with. But, in spite of this, he had something in him which all the finest people he met recognized as superior. Madame Von Breuning saw, plainly enough, that his faults were only on the surface. She had discernment enough to perceive that underneath the uncouth exterior and bearish behavior of this rude and violent youth there lay the essentials of a noble character. She respected him accordingly, liked

His manners and character.

him in spite of his faults, admitted him to the intimate friendship of herself and her family, encouraged him in every way, and introduced him to the best German and English literature. Here he formed intellectual and literary tastes which were of the highest importance in his development, and which lasted him throughout his life. Meanwhile, his father went from bad to worse, and at last fell so low, that before Ludwig was nineteen years old, the Elector ordered a part of his father's salary to be paid over to him, and he thus became, in a way, his father's guardian, and the real head of the family.

He remained at Bonn, in the service of the Elector, in intimate association with the friends already mentioned, and constantly engaged in composition, until November, 1792. He was now nearly twenty-two years old. Compared with Mozart's productions at that age, the pieces he had composed were few in number, small and unimportant; but there were already to be found in them hints of his future greatness, and suggestions of what was to be the distinctive characteristic of his future works, grandeur and sublimity, nobility and elevation of emotional content, and a profundity and force of passion such as had been hitherto unknown in the works of any composer. His acquaintances were impressed with his powers, and believed in his genius, but this impression was probably due much more to the fire, imagination and force of his playing than to anything in his compositions, for in improvisation he is said to have surpassed even Mozart. We have al-

CHAP. VI.

ready seen that his extemporaneous playing made a profound impression on Mozart, at Beethoven's first visit to Vienna, and Haydn was similarly impressed when he passed through Bonn, on his way to London, in December, 1790, and again on his return in July, 1792. The high opinion which Haydn formed of Beethoven's talent, finally resulted in the young man's going to Vienna to study with the old composer, in November, 1792, and thenceforth Beethoven lived in Vienna until his death.

Lessons with Haydn.

But his lessons with Haydn were a disappointment. Haydn was very busy, and seems to have neglected his pupil somewhat; but besides, it soon became clear that the natures of the two men were so incompatible that the relation of teacher and pupil could be hardly pleasant or profitable to either. Each was original in his way, but the ways were radically different. Haydn himself had been an innovator, had opened up new fields, and by breaking new paths for himself had aroused the antagonism of the pedants of his day. Beethoven was to be equally a pioneer in unexplored regions, and was equally to incur the hostility not only of pedantic worshippers of "the letter which killeth," but even the disapproval of Haydn, genius though he was. Haydn had never hesitated to break the rules of the old contrapuntists whenever he thought he could produce a better effect by so doing. He was conscious of an unerring insight which enabled him to discover principles beyond the ken of the musical grammarians and purists of his time. It is probable that, on general principles, he would not have disapproved of any young composer's taking a similar course, for Haydn was catholic in his views; but he was now an old man and seems to have been incapable of comprehending the new spirit which impelled his vigorous young pupil in a direction wholly different from that which he himself had taken, and almost as widely divergent from the course of Mozart, whom Haydn fully understood and appreciated. When Beethoven submitted his first three Trios to Haydn's criticism, the old man frankly advised him not to publish the third. Beethoven knew this to be the best of the three, and such an opinion of course destroyed the young composer's confidence in the critical judgment of his teacher, for Beethoven's intuitions were sure, and he walked no uncertain road. Diverge from Haydn he must and did; and the necessity prevented all intimacy and cordial personal relations, though there was never any open quarrel. Haydn seems to have mildly resented young Beethoven's unteachableness and lack of proper respect, while Ludwig expressed his disregard for Haydn's opinions with a good deal of frankness.

Thus Haydn's formal instruction of the new genius amounted to but very little. Beethoven took lessons of others, especially of Albrechtsberger, the great contrapuntist, but he assimilated their teachings in his own way, formed ideals of his own totally different from those set before him by his teachers, used their lessons merely as hints for orig-

CHAP. VI.

Acknowl-
edgment
of his
claims by
the
amateurs
of Vienna.

inal discoveries incomprehensible to them, and as material for the accomplishment of results which, though now long since accepted as valid, awakened in them only disapproval and contempt.

"Have nothing to do with him," said Albrechtsberger to a young student, "he has learnt nothing, and will never do anything in decent style." But though learned pedants and dry contrapuntists could not see the dawning greatness of a genius of the first rank, it was plain enough to the noble and cultivated amateurs whose patronage was at that time the only support of artists in Vienna. Beethoven at once acquired friends, admirers and patrons among the Austrian aristocracy. The Prince Lichnowsky and Baron van Swieten at first, and after them nearly all the aristocratic connoisseurs of the music-loving capital, employed him at private concerts and as a teacher, bought his compositions, furnished him players to try his quartets and trios over before they were finished, received him into their houses on the most intimate terms and in every way showed their appreciation of his talents and his character. He was soon thrown on his own resources by the withdrawal of his allowance from Bonn, and henceforth he supported himself by composition, concerts and teaching. That he should have found no difficulty in doing so is not so surprising, although it is certainly creditable to his patrons that they should have discerned in him abilities as a musician which his teachers had failed to see.

What is astonishing, on the surface, is Beethoven's personal relations to this high-born society. It would doubtless have been entirely possible for his aristocratic patrons to have shown their appreciation of his musical gifts and attainments, and to have supported him liberally, without admitting him to social intercourse, for which, by his birth, his education, his personal habits and his outward behavior, he was every way unfitted, and so remained to the last.

His personal relations to the highborn society of Vienna.

He was absent-minded and careless of his dress to the last degree; he was untidy, not to say unkempt and dirty; his table manners were almost intolerable; he would come into an elegant drawing-room after walking in the rain and shake the water from his hat over the furniture, oblivious of any possibility of damage; he was perpetually breaking whatever he touched; he was extremely sensitive, irritable, violent and abusive; he stormed at his pupils, young ladies of the highest rank; he insulted the gentlemen whose guest he was; in short, his outward behavior might not inaptly be summed up in the sailor's verdict on the cannibals: "Manners they have none, and their customs are disgusting."

His dress, manners and behavior.

Moreover, the social distance between noble families and such as his was at that time very great indeed. Yet he was received on terms of equality into an aristocratic society as elegant and refined as any in Europe; was admired and loved equally by gentlemen and ladies; his faults were overlooked; his boorishness and abuse were submitted to, and

Chap. VI.
His social success accounted for.

he was treated in all respects as if he honored that society by his presence. To account for this phenomenon it is not sufficient to point to the evidences of his musical genius, for neither Haydn nor Mozart, though both original geniuses, and, moreover, gentlemen in demeanor, were treated with such consideration by this same society. The truth is, that Beethoven's faults were merely superficial. They were hard enough to tolerate in elegant society, or indeed in any company, but they did not by any means touch the foundation of his character. His neglect of dress, and of good table habits, of the minor moralities and the amenities of social intercourse were due partly to lack of early training, and still more to his complete mental absorption in the ideal conceptions which always filled his imagination, and which have become the world's precious possessions.

His irritability only upon the surface.

His irritability and violent explosions of ungovernable rage were largely due to the same cause; for, with a nervous constitution sensitive and excitable in the extreme, any interruption of his preoccupation, especially any disagreeable interference with the flow of his ideas, was a rude shock which roused sudden and violent resentment. But though he was not very considerate of other people's rights and feelings in minor matters, in greater ones it was not so. If he did not tithe the mint, anise and cummin, he did not neglect the weightier matters of the law. The surface of his behavior was often ruffled by gusts of ill-temper, but the depths of his soul remained in profound quiet. And depths there were, and heights, too, in the soul of this man, such as few could measure or fathom; a profundity of passion, a loftiness of thinking, a nobility of feeling, an elevation of purpose such as commanded the respect of all discerning persons.

Doubtless this alone would not account for his relations to the Vienna aristocracy, any more than his musical gifts and attainments would be sufficient. But the central point is that *Beethoven's music embodied all that was noblest and best in his character.* It was not mere arrangement and combination of sounds for amusement; it was not even merely the creation of beautiful forms, for the gratification of a high æsthetic taste; it was the embodiment of emotional experiences which could only have been possible to a man of the highest intellectual endowments, the profoundest capacity of feeling, whose thoughts and emotions and purposes were ideally pure and noble.

Beethoven took his art seriously; as seriously as a saint and martyr takes his religion. To him it involved right living; it was a perpetual consecration. The fire of his enthusiasm burned continually without abatement. This consecration, this absolute devotion to ideal aims was the attraction which drew to him the noblest, the purest, the most refined of the men and women of the time and place in which he lived; and this it is which gives him a place among the highest in the love and the esteem of the best of our day.

His immortality as a composer is due mainly to the nobility of the content of his compositions. His

CHAP. VI.
Why he is an immortal composer.

sonatas, symphonies, trios and quartets are indeed master-pieces in form and style; but Form, with Beethoven, was not the most important matter. The classical form of the sonata had already reached its culmination in Haydn and Mozart. Beethoven accepted this form, without question, as it came from the hands of his elder contemporaries, and soon began to manifest his originality by filling it with a new emotional content. The very first of his pianoforte sonatas are superior to the best of Mozart's in point of significance. Indeed, the adagio of his first sonata, in F minor, op. 2, is incomparably more beautiful than anything of the kind which had preceded it, and this beauty is due, not to greater perfection of form, not to superior elegance or grace of style, but to its noble serenity of spirit, "a peace that passeth understanding," peace which comes from the consciousness of union with the Highest, the repose won by self-conquest, by struggle and victory.

Content of Haydn's music.

In Haydn's pianoforte compositions there reigns the cheerfulness of child-like innocence, perpetual freshness of spirit, with no evidence of any heights or depths of passion, of struggle with temptation or with fate, or any knowledge of evil, profound sorrow or suffering. For aught that appears in most of them he might always have retained the feelings of a healthy, good-natured, careless child, at play in the sunshine. And this was doubtless the spirit in which he habitually wrote. He had annoyances and troubles but instead of seeking to express his troubled feelings in music he used his art as a refuge from all things unpleasant, forgetting them in the creation of beautiful forms and combinations, into which he always infused a cheerful mood. At least there was seldom anything more divergent from this than a mild melancholy, introduced for the sake of enhancing the gayer mood by contrast. In Mozart the characteristic mood is gayety, keen enjoyment, a never-failing appetite for pleasure; but the sources of this pleasure are not so simple. He is more many-sided; has had a wider experience of men and things; has vastly more impressions to reproduce. Into his short thirty-five years were crowded a richness and variety of social and musical experience, from his life in the pleasure-loving Austrian capital, in comparison with which, Haydn's quiet, retired life at Prince Esterhazy's country seat, occupied in composing for his own small orchestra and choir, was simplicity itself.

Accordingly, we find in Mozart's music, as the unconscious reproduction of his emotional life, a many-sidedness, a variety and richness, especially in the coloring of his orchestral compositions, to which his older contemporary can lay no claim. But in all this there is little of grandeur or sublimity. Grace, there is, consummate ease and elegance, the polish of a complete man of the world, who is perfectly at home in all elegant society, gives himself up to his daily pleasures with the frank and hearty abandon of a boy, accepts life as he finds it, and never troubles his head with its deeper and

Chap. VI.

Content of Mozart's music.

CHAP. VI.

Neither Hadyn nor Mozart frivolous.

Content in the instrumental music of both a subordinate matter.

Haydn's attempts at dramatic characterization.

sadder problems, and whose good-humor, zest for pleasure and buoyancy of spirits, nothing can overcome.

Not indeed that the music of either Haydn or Mozart is frivolous or shallow, far from it. To both, music was a serious occupation, an exalted pleasure, and, barring some few things written from the necessity of earning money, and lacking the true inspiration, the ruling motive seems to have been to embody an ideal of beauty conditioned on sensuously beautiful tones combined into logical forms. This music is not only not trivial, but often has a noble emotional significance. The ruling mood in it seems to be the keen pleasure experienced by the composer in the contemplation of his own beautiful conception, and in the work of artistic creation. This refers more especially to the purely instrumental compositions of both. When they had to deal with words, they embodied the emotions raised by the ideas of the text. This they did, doubtless, intuitively and in a sense unconsciously. It is not probable that either of them philosophized much, if at all, about the relation of music to emotion, and its proper limits as a means of emotional expression. But they both instinctively felt what was fitting in the relation of their music to the words chosen.

There are indeed instances, such as the peculiar figure in "The Creation" at the words, "With sudden leap the flexible tiger appears," and other similar cases in the same work, which almost look like crude attempts to "depict" the leap of the tiger, etc., but everywhere Haydn is saved, by innate refinement of perception, from the fatal step which would land him in the ridiculous.

The operas of Mozart are full of admirable examples of dramatic characterization. Indeed, neither Haydn nor Mozart appears at his best in his pianoforte music; a fact doubtless due, at least in part, to the limitations and imperfections of the instrument in their time. When they deal with the orchestra or with voices, the content of their music becomes nobler and more characteristic. Still, in the instrumental compositions, the form seems always to have been a prime consideration, and neither seems to have attempted or even desired to embody a content which could not be perfectly expressed through the form of the sonata.

With Beethoven the case was different. His was a larger, deeper, more powerful nature, with superabundance of untamed energy. He was saturated with the great ideas of his time, the time of the French Revolution; he was independent to the last degree, carrying his contempt for old forms and etiquette to an extreme which accounts for much of his rudeness of behavior. He would have no social shams, no cant, no hypocrisy, no putting the best side out, no shallow compliments, no superiority except such as was created by character and gifts. Was his brother Johann a "property owner?" He was a "brain owner." Had the Austrian Emperor and nobles, title, rank, wealth? He had what rank could not give nor money purchase, the genius and

Beethoven's character and ideals.

CHAP. VI.

His ideals find expression in music.

Classical forms modified to suit the content embodied in them.

gifts which God had bestowed upon him, and he not only asserted but forced acknowledgment of his equality with the proudest of the aristocracy. The great ideas of Liberty, Equality, Fraternity, filled and inspired him with emotions unknown to his predecessors.

If these ideas and feelings found mistaken and unworthy forms of expression in his outward behavior, they came to the noblest and most inspiring embodiment in his great compositions. Witness the Symphony "Eroica," the Fifth and Ninth Symphonies, the "Sonata Appassionata," the Sonatas from op. 101 to op. 111, as conspicuous examples.

This new and superior emotional content had a marked effect on the formal construction of his compositions. He did indeed write sonatas to the end of his life, but he modified the form to suit the content which he had to express and for which the somewhat stiff and formal outlines of the classic sonata were no longer adapted. Neither Haydn nor Mozart seemed to have anything to say which could not be said while giving supreme place to classical symmetry of form, balance of nearly related keys and uniformity of plan in a whole series of works. What Beethoven had to say required greater freedom in the treatment of themes, greater variety in keys and frequency of abrupt modulation, and not seldom departures from the traditional proportions of the principal and subordinate groups. These modifications are no contribution to the completion of the classical form; that was already perfect; that ideal had already been realized; they were departures from the classical in the direction of the Romantic ideal. To quote an able writer:* "None of these alterations and additions to the usual forms were made by Beethoven for their own sake. They were made because he had something to say on his subject which the rules did not give him time and space to say, and which he could not leave unsaid. His work is a poem, in which the thoughts and emotions are the first things, and the forms of expression second and subordinate.'

This intellectual and emotional content is admirably characterized by Mr. Edward Dannreuther in an article quoted by Mr. Grove. "While listening to such works as the Overture to Leonora, the Sinfonia Eroica, or the Ninth Symphony, we feel that we are in the presence of something far wider and higher than the mere development of musical themes. The execution in detail of each movement and each succeeding work is modified more and more with the prevailing poetic sentiment. A religious passion and elevation are present in the utterances. The mental and moral horizon of the music grows upon us with each new hearing. The different movements, like the different particles of each movement, have as close a connection with each other as the acts of a tragedy, and a characteristic significance to be understood only in relation

*See Grove's Dictionary of Music and Musicians, article Beethoven, page 207.

Dannreuther's estimate of his music.

CHAP. VI.

The ethical quality of his music.

First publications.

to the whole ; each work is in the full sense of the word a revelation.

" Beethoven speaks a language no one has spoken before, and treats of things no one has dreamt of before ; yet it seems as though he were speaking of matters long familiar, in one's mother-tongue ; as though he touched upon emotions one had lived through in some former existence. The warmth and depth of his ethical sentiment is now felt all the world over, and it will ere long be universally recognized that he has leavened and widened the sphere of men's emotions in a manner akin to that in which the conceptions of great philosophers and poets have widened the sphere of men's intellectual activity."

Having sought to account for Beethoven's relations to the society in which he lived, by giving some notion of his character and works, it is now time to return to the narrative of his life, which shall be briefly sketched. Our digression began at the point when he had come to settle in Vienna, had been taken up by Prince Lichnowsky and Baron von Swieten, and was taking lessons of Haydn and Albrechtsberger. This was in 1792. His studies in composition began to bear excellent fruit in about three years. In July, 1795, were published his three pianoforte trios, op. 1, and soon afterward the three pianoforte sonatas, op. 2. These works were evidently modelled on Haydn and Mozart, the best composers of his time, but they are original and characteristic. They excited much enthusiasm, one evidence of which is the proposal made to him by Count Appony to write a string quartet at his own price.

First and second concertos.

Before and during this year he had also written several of his minor compositions for the pianoforte, and what is of more importance, his first and second concertos. The concerto in C major he played at a concert in the Burg theater given for the benefit of a widow's fund of the Artist's Society, and surprised the musicians by the feat of playing it in C sharp, the pianoforte being a half tone flat. He also played at other concerts this year, one of them Haydn's.

The sonata in E flat, op. 7.

The record of 1796 is much the same. The most significant compositions of this year were the pianoforte Sonata in E flat, op. 7, so markedly original as to create a new epoch in pianoforte music, and the quintet for piano and wind instruments, op. 16. He continued to grow steadily from year to year. Most of his compositions for some time naturally fell below the mark he had reached in the E flat Sonata in point of originality, but they were all significant, and the Sonata, op. 10, No. 3, written in 1798, is an important landmark in his progress. In 1797, his noble love-song, "Adelaide," was written. His work in composition was varied by concerts and much private playing. He used to meet his brother musicians and engage in friendly trials of skill. In one of these encounters, not so friendly, he worsted Steibelt, who was very jealous of him, by taking the violoncello part of Steibelt's new quintet, turning it

Friendly trials of skill.

upside down, and improvising on the theme thus obtained so brilliantly that Steibelt was fairly driven from the room. His frequent meetings with Woefl were more satisfactory. Both were excellent players and improvisators, and both thoroughly enjoyed their frequent musical contests.

Larger works.

Beethoven soon began to plan larger works. "The Sonata pathetique" was written in 1799, and a beginning was made on the string quartets, op. 18, the septet, the first symphony, and his oratorio, "The Mount of Olives." His pianoforte sonata in B flat, op. 22, was also begun about this time, and the third concerto in C minor, followed very soon. All through the first year of the present century he was absorbed in these works and in conceiving new ones, though "The Mount of Olives" was not finished for some years. His mental activity was incessant. The list of all his works and the details concerning them would occupy more space than can be given them in this chapter. Only salient points which serve to trace his mental growth and the development of his genius can here be indicated.

Sonatas, op. 26-27.

Among the pianoforte compositions, which more immediately concern us, there were the sonatas in A flat, op. 26, the two sonatas, op. 27, of which the one in C sharp minor, commonly known as the "Moonlight," is among the most original of all his works, and the so-called "Pastoral" sonata, op. 28, all of which belong to the year 1800.

But he was now becoming seriously deaf. For some time he had suffered from violent noises in his ears, and the case was rapidly growing worse. Many physicians were consulted, but none of them could help him. At thirty years old, this greatest of musicians and composers was looking forward to the prospect of being unable to hear a single note. The key-note of his character is given in the following quotation from a letter of his, which shows how he faced it : " I will, as far as possible, defy my fate, though there must be moments when I shall be the most miserable of God's creatures. Not unhappy, no ; that I could never endure. I will grapple with fate ; it never shall drag me down." This is the mood of the "sonata appassionata," a sonata which must always remain one of the noblest of human utterances, the revelation of a high soul, subjected to suffering the most intense, yet unconquered and unconquerable.

His deafness.

In spite of his sufferings and his apprehensions he worked on diligently. He commonly had several new compositions in his mind at once, turned them over and over, sketched them slowly, elaborated them laboriously, and only by slow degrees did any of them grow to completeness. The spontaneity and marvelous rapidity of production which strike us so forcibly in Mozart were never characteristic of Beethoven, but the works which grew in his mind so slowly attained majestic proportions and overtopped those of Mozart as the slow-growing, lofty oak towers above the graceful birch or the quick-growing aspen.

His industry.

The sonatas above referred to already had much

Chap. VI.

Sonatas, op. 31.

of this loftiness of character. The year 1803 saw another step in his development, the production of the sonatas, op. 31, in which he himself recognized a change in his style; he also wrote the three violin sonatas, op. 30, and some minor compositions. But the most important work which occupied him at this time was his Third Symphony, the "Eroica," the inspiration of which is drawn from the noblest ideas which underlay the French Revolution, and from the career of Napoleon Bonaparte up to the time of his assuming the title of Emperor. The work was already finished and dedicated to Napoleon when the news of this event came to Vienna. Beethoven tore off the title page and dashed it on the floor in a rage.

The next year his one noble opera, "Fidelio," was written, and other important compositions, which can not here be dwelt upon, followed rapidly. Full details are to be found in Grove's Dictionary and elsewhere.

Farther anxiety.

So it went on until 1815, when his brother Casper died, and this event was the beginning of the last epoch in Beethoven's life. Casper left his son Carl, then some eight years old, to the care of his brother, and as the boy turned out wholly worthless, he became a constant source of worry and anxiety to his already overburdened uncle.

The case was further complicated by the fact that Carl's mother was determined to get possession of him, and contested Beethoven's right to him in the courts, while Ludwig regarded his sister-in-law as a disreputable person, unfit to have charge of her son, and resolutely declined to allow her to have anything to do with him. The added sorrow and vexation which these untoward circumstances caused the composer, must have hindered his work and hastened the exhaustion of his powers, but he worked on, bravely and steadily, produced and published his great works for pianoforte, his chamber music, symphonies, etc., one after another, while his deafness grew upon him, his domestic griefs and anxiety increased, and his health gradually failed. It became impossible for him to hear even the loudest notes of the orchestra, and all communication with him had to be in writing.

He becomes totally deaf.

But it is doubtless due partly to these very circumstances, apparently so unfavorable, that this latter period of Beethoven's life was rich in the noblest and most original of his compositions. His music was the expression of his emotional experience, and this experience was deepened, purified, exalted, ennobled, by the fires of affliction. "It is only fire that takes out dross," and out of the furnace came the real gold of Beethoven's character. What he was, in his inmost soul, that his music shows. What was mean in his externals or rude in his behavior was mere husk; the real heart of him is in the Sonata, op. 111 and the Ninth Symphony.

Last works.

The terrible trials out of which these works grew, continued for twelve years, and then came the end. His worthless nephew made him much trouble, finally attempted suicide, and was ordered out of Vienna by the police. Beethoven went with the boy to his brother Johann's in the country. Here he and Johann had a tiff, and he returned to Vienna in bad weather, took cold, soon had inflammation of the lungs and then dropsy. He never rose from this sickness, but died on the 26th of March, 1827.

CHAPTER VII.

The Transition from the Classic to the Romantic Period.

THE CLASSIC AND THE ROMANTIC IN MUSIC.

The term "classic" is used in two senses. In the one sense it means—having permanent interest and value—and is thus contrasted with the evanescent and the ephemeral. In this sense any composition is a classic which succeeds in maintaining its place in the interest of mankind for ages after the death of its author. No one can certainly determine during the lifetime of any composer whether his works are classics in this sense or not, because the only sure test is that of time. We may, indeed, have reason to think that a given work of excellence possesses elements of permanent and universal interest, but in such matters it is easy to be misled, and the history of music and of literature affords innumerable instances of errors in judgment as regards this point on the part of critics and connoisseurs. We can not, therefore, safely predicate the term "classic" in the first sense of any contemporary works. Whatever has come down to us from a period sufficiently remote to show that the interest it awakens is permanent, that the world will not willingly let it die,

marginal note: CHAP. VII. *The term "classic" defined.*

CHAP. VII.

Classic and romantic ideals contrasted.

Relation of form to content

is classic; nothing else is, though many among contemporary works may possibly become so.

In the second sense, the term "classic," or, more commonly, "classical," is used to designate music written in a particular style, aiming at the embodiment of a certain ideal, the chief element of which is Beauty of Form. In this sense it is contrasted with the term "Romantic," a term used to designate music which aims at embodying a different ideal, that of the vivid and truthful expression of varied and strongly contrasted emotional experiences, such as we are accustomed to connect with the word "romantic" in literature and in life.

In "classical" music, in this sense, Form is first and content is subordinate; in "romantic" music content is first and Form is subordinate. The classical ideal is predominantly an intellectual one. Its products are characterized by clearness of thought, by completeness and symmetry, by harmonious proportion, by simplicity and repose. Classical works, whether musical or literary, are positive, clear, finished. The following axioms from Aristotle's "Poetics" (quoted in the New American Cyclopedia, article "classics",) apply quite as well to classical music as to Greek poetry. "There is nothing beautiful in literature nor the arts which may not be clearly analyzed by the intellect." "Every poem must be contained within prescribed boundaries, so that it may be easy for the mind to embrace it at a single glance, and to form a single conception or picture of it."

These are the fundamental principles which underlie all classical compositions.

Chap. VII.

It is easy to see that, up to Beethoven's time, the classical ideal had been predominant, at least in pianoforte music. Indeed, no other had come forward with any prominence. There were sporadic cases which did not conform to the classical ideal, but there was no other style generally recognized or sought after.

The classical ideal predominant before Beethoven.

The Bach fugues, in which the polyphonic mode of writing culminated, and the Mozart sonatas, concertos, quartets, and symphonies, in which the limit of development of monophonic Form was reached, have all the characteristics above described. They are, indeed, often long and complex, composed of many parts, developed to an extent unknown to earlier composers, but their plan is always simple and easily grasped as a whole and in its details, it is strictly logical, it has the most perfect unity of idea, its parts are symmetrically balanced, the proportions are simple, the modulations are confined to a narrow range of nearly related keys for the sake of simplicity and clearness; in short, the composer laid all possible stress on the necessity of producing beautiful, clearly intelligible works, satisfactory to the intellect and to the logical sense.

This being the case, it is obvious that the emotional content of them must necessarily have been simple. A composer whose mind is mainly occupied with the intellectual side of his work, who aims primarily at clearness of statement as the main con-

The emotional content of the classical works simple.

dition of formal beauty, can not at the same time be agitated by violent and contending passions, or disturbed by vague yearnings or urgent desires. The emotional content of his forms must be simple and reposeful, such as simple pleasure or sadness, elevated joy in the contemplation of grandeur, or melancholy of a mild type. The simpler emotional experiences alone were adapted for expression through the strictly classical forms, and accordingly we find no other in the works of the composers above referred to, or in those of their contemporaries.

Imagination there is in their works, and that of the finest type, but it deals with its musical materials solely with reference to an Ideal of Beauty, of which the expression of violent and conflicting emotions formed no part, and to which such emotions were not only foreign but antagonistic. It is characteristic, too, that not only were simple emotions, or moods, more or less indefinite or vague, the sole content admissible in their mode of writing, but that these moods in their successions and relations were, like the form of the compositions, developed in a logical way, were conceived as under rational control and subordinate to intelligence. They were, in short, the natural expressions of the emotional life of healthy, simple, natural, well-regulated minds, living in the present, engrossed mainly with present enjoyments more or less refined, and wholly free from disquieting questions, and from unrest of every sort.

The moods were logically developed.

With Beethoven the case was different. His mental and moral horizon was wider, his aspirations higher, his sympathies stronger and more intense, his joys and sorrows struck deeper root in profounder soil, and spread their branches in loftier and purer air, receiving more of sunshine and casting deeper shadow.

In all the great artists there has been prominent the conception of the Beautiful as a manifestation of the Divine, and therefore as closely connected with ideals of religion and morality. The perception of this is their greatest claim to be seers and prophets for the race. But with Beethoven this was pre-eminently the case. The "religious passion and elevation" quoted from Mr. Dannreuther in the last chapter, is the key-note of his character, and he was a musician and not something else, because he found in his chosen art the most perfect medium in which to embody his most characteristic ideals and feelings.

He was powerfully affected by the French Revolution, and gave a passionate response to the great ideas which gave rise to it. But he was also strongly influenced by his study of English literature and of the German school of Romantic Poetry, with both of which he became acquainted in his youth, in the house of Madame von Breuning. This latter school was made up of young men, his contemporaries, and aimed at nothing less than freeing German Poetry from the shackles of a blind imitation of the stiff and affected pseudo classicism of France.

French literature had up to this time been predominant in German thought, and its stilted forms had served as the only accepted models for German writers.

Characteristics of the German romantic writers.

The young writers of the new school discarded the current rules, sought their models and subjects in the middle age romances, laid all possible stress on the vivid representation of natural feelings in their most vigorous manifestations and little or none on conventional rules or established principles of composition. They dealt in violent passions, in strongly contrasted situations, in weird and fantastic images. They put desire and yearning in the place of present enjoyment; vague mysticism in the place of definite clearness of ideas; well-defined, powerful feelings in the place of simple, vague moods.

It is probable that Beethoven did not definitely propose to himself to attempt in music the same sort of revolution which Tieck, the Schlegels and others were accomplishing in German literature. Very likely he did little or no philosophizing on the subject; but he was strongly influenced by the intellectual movements of his time, with what result we have already seen. He proclaimed no new revolutionary gospel in the forms of composition. Outwardly, he conformed to the classical school, just as he nominally belonged to the Roman Catholic Church. But in both cases the inward spirit is too great for the form in which it is contained.

The Romantic School really began with Beethoven, and his example and character gave it its most powerful impulse, though there is, perhaps, not a word to be quoted from him in direct advocacy of the new principle.

The romantic school of music begins with him.

It was left to the young men of the next generation to devote themselves with full consciousness of their own aims to the promotion of the principles which underlay his practice, to fight the battle of "David against the Philistines," and to establish the supremacy of the nobler aspirations of human nature, of the unrest of dissatisfaction with imperfection and wrong, of yearning and outreaching desire for better things, of agitated striving, of resistance, struggle and conquest as motives in art, as against simple, childlike pleasure and pain, quiet repose and harmonious beauty.

Two great contemporaries of Beethoven shared the influences which affected him, and with him prepared the way for the romantic composers proper; to them the next chapter will be devoted.

CHAPTER VIII.

BEETHOVEN'S TWO GREATEST CONTEMPORARIES IN
THE DOMAIN OF PIANOFORTE MUSIC.
CARL MARIA VON WEBER (1786-1826).
FRANZ PETER SCHUBERT (1797-1828).

CHAP. VIII.
C. M. von Weber.

CARL MARIA VON WEBER was born at Eutin, in Holstein, December 18, 1786. He came of a family in whom the love of music, and still more the love of the drama, had been prominent traits. In some of them, indeed, these two impulses had become consuming passions. The boy's father, Franz Anton, was one of these. He does not seem to have possessed remarkable abilities, either histrionic or musical, and had had excellent opportunities to rise in the world in other callings; but his innate tendencies toward music and the stage impelled him irresistibly into the life of a strolling player and

His childhood surroundings.

musician. Into this life, irregular, unhealthful for mind and body, he dragged his unwilling family, to the disgust and shame of his wife, and the detriment of his children.

None of the family displayed remarkable talents, or gave any promise of realizing Franz Anton's dream of giving to the world another musical genius like Mozart, except Carl Maria. In this boy, all the artistic life of the family for long generations seems to have been gathered up and to have reached its culmination. Franz Anton, wild, wayward, impulsive, reckless, incapable of steadiness of purpose or of sustained thinking, was by no means a desirable guide and tutor for a young artist, and all the surroundings of the boy's childhood and early youth were such as tended toward mental dissipation. All through his life, Weber felt the effects of these disadvantages, in his incapacity for mental concentration and sustained intellectual exertion, and was obliged, in middle life, to subject himself to the severest discipline in order to counteract, so far as might be, the defects of his early training. He was a weak, nervous child, with a disease of the thigh bone which caused him to limp and withdrew him in great measure from the sports of his playmates. Sensitive and impressible, his father's persistent and injudicious attempts to force him to become a youthful prodigy, excited in him only disgust with art, and for a long time he accomplished very little. Such interest as he acquired in music came not through his father's ill-judged exertions, but mainly through the sound, discreet and sympathetic instruction of two men, J. P. Henschkel, of Hildburghausen, and Michael Haydn, of Salzburg. In both these places the wandering family stopped long enough to give the poor child some little chance of proper instruction. But one benefit he did undoubtedly derive from his father's profession. From his earliest childhood he was familiar with theatrical representations and stage effects, and this

Chap. VIII.

Carl's gifts.

His weak, nervous constitution.

His teachers.

familiarity was afterwards of incalculable advantage to him as an operatic composer.

In spite of the irregularities of his instruction, he made considerable progress in piano-playing, and finally attained distinction as a brilliant and effective concert pianist. This result, as well as the more solid development of his skill and his gifts as a composer, was attained in Vienna, where he lived from his fourteenth until his eighteenth year. He became a pupil of the Abbé Vogler, then a highly esteemed composer and teacher, a man of some really solid attainments and ability and of admirable tact. He had, indeed, faults which resembled those of Carl's father. He was vain and given to show, ready to buy a brilliant and seeming success with showy and superficial accomplishments. It is no wonder that the boy should have been injured by the commanding influence of two such men. His vanity and over-sensitiveness to praise were continually fostered, and the damage would have been worse if Franz Anton's foolish bragging and overweening vanity had not been so boundless that the lad was fairly disgusted, and experienced something of a wholesome reaction against it.

But these were not the only dangers which beset the gifted youth. Vienna was a gay, dissipated, pleasure-loving capital. Carl's mother was dead, and there was little to restrain him from yielding to temptations which inevitably allured him on all sides. His most intimate friend was a young ex-officer named Gaensbacher, who was also studying under the Abbé Vogler, an enthusiastic lover and student of music, but given to all sorts of illicit indulgences. With him and his set young Carl lived a fast, irregular life, quaffing eagerly the cup of pleasure. Nevertheless, he did a good deal of real work, and profited not a little by his instruction as well as by the multitudinous impressions he received in a city which had been for more than fifty years the musical capital of Europe, where Mozart had lived and worked, where Haydn still dwelt in his old age, and where Beethoven was making a most profound impression.

Before he was quite eighteen years old, he was called, on the recommendation of the Abbé Vogler, to be conductor of the opera in Breslau. He showed marked talent in his new position of responsibility, and gained invaluable experience. But he also showed conceit enough to rouse a great deal of enmity, and he continued the career of dissipation he had begun in Vienna. At the end of two years he was overwhelmed with debt, and besides had so much opposition to encounter in his work that he abandoned his post in disgust.

This was in 1806, and the armies of Napoleon were already overrunning the country. Murder, rapine, outrages of all sorts were daily perpetrated, the public mind became wholly occupied with the war, and artists fared hard. Weber was, for a time, the guest of Prince Eugene, of Wuertemberg, at Carlsruhe, but was driven from this asylum by the disorders of the time. Prince Eugene obtained for him the position of private secretary to his brother, Duke Ludwig, at Stuttgart, where still another brother, Friedrich, was reigning King. Friedrich was a coarse, passionate man, violent in his temper and manners, and, as a ruler, arbitrary and tyrannical; his brother, Weber's patron, was not only weak and self-indulgent, but also dissolute and reckless; the whole court and society in which the young man was thrown was utterly corrupt and venal, and wholly given up to the coarsest immorality. It is not to be wondered at that a youth of his antecedents should have plunged even deeper than ever before into dissipation and debauchery. He finished sowing his wild oats in Stuttgart, and began reaping the very disagreeable crop which came of them.

But there were redeeming traits in the young man, and redeeming influences in Stuttgart society. There were excellent families there, and some literary men and artists, who exercised a wholesome and saving influence on Carl Maria. The man whose sterling worth and devoted friendship was of most value to him was Franz Danzi, conductor of the Royal Opera, a sound musician, an admirable man, full of high ideals, with penetration enough to see what latent possibilities lay in the young composer, with a strong desire to develop them, and with tact enough to win Weber's confidence and affection, though he was more than double his age. One of his great maxims was, "To be a true artist, you must be a true man;" and he exerted all his influence to stem the tide of sinful indulgences on which his weak young friend was floating, to call forth his latent moral sense, to awaken his conscience, his desire for intellectual attainments and artistic achievements; in short, to make of him such a man and artist as he knew him to be capable of becoming.

But these lessons were not to have their full effect until Weber had had the sharp schooling of adversity. The end came in the early part of 1810. The young private secretary had long been under the King's displeasure; he was now arrested, thrown into prison, and soon banished from Wuertemberg, —turned out in poverty, to get on as best he could. Henceforth he became a man; with numerous weaknesses, indeed, heavily handicapped by his inherited traits and tendencies and by his youthful follies; but conscious of both his weakness and his strength, and fully determined to make the most of himself for the rest of his life.

The next three years he spent in wandering about through Germany and Switzerland, supporting himself by giving concerts, by the sale of his compositions, and by critical work. He had studied philosophy and æsthetics in Vienna, had shown intellectual powers of a high order, decided ability as a critic, and had developed an effective literary style. His critical writings were sought by the best musical journals of Germany, and he wrote a great deal, especially during his stay in Berlin and in Leipsic. His operas "Sylvana" and "Abu Hassan," as well as his cantata "The First Tone," had already been composed at Stuttgart, and these were now successfully given in many places. His songs also brought him reputation and money. His piano-playing awakened great admiration. It was brilliant and effective, characterized by perfect mastery of the instrument, by extraordinary execution, and especially in improvisation he showed such command of the resources of harmony and such power of expressing his feelings, that he is said to have produced "a marvellous effect, such as had never been hitherto known in the art of piano-playing."* This naturally led to the sale of his pianoforte compositions.

During his wanderings he received a great variety of impressions of men and things, associated with many artists, poets and intellectual men of high standing, as well as with persons of the highest social rank, acquired wide experience of music, literature and life, worked hard to improve himself as composer and man, and gained every way in character, in knowledge, in manysidedness, in concentration and in command of his own powers.

Early in 1813 he accepted the conductorship of the opera at Prague, and was once more settled for some time. His work in this position lasted till October, 1816, somewhat more than three years and a half. It was a time of hard work, of struggle and discipline, of weakness, but also of growth in self-mastery. Weber's work as a conductor was efficient and successful. His production seems to have been mainly limited to his patriotic songs, which excited

---

*See letter of his friend Lichtenstein, quoted in Life of Weber, by his son, Vol. I, pages 206-7.

the greatest enthusiasm throughout Germany. To these must be added his important cantata, "Battle and Victory," written in celebration of the overthrow of Napoleon at Waterloo.

On Christmas day, 1816, he received the appointment of conductor to his majesty the King of Saxony, and thenceforth the remaining ten years of his life were to be devoted to the establishment of German opera at Dresden. This portion of his life must be here sketched in the briefest possible manner. Full details are to be found in Weber's Life, by his son, already referred to.

The three great romantic operas which made Weber's name immortal were composed during his life in Dresden. "Der Freischuetz" was produced for his own theatre in 1820, but was first given successfully in Berlin; "Euryanthe" was written for Vienna in 1822; and "Oberon" for London in 1825. To these must be added his music to "Preciosa," also written in 1820. He went to London to superintend the performances of "Oberon," and died there of consumption, January 4, 1826.

Weber's place in musical history depends mainly on his three great operas mentioned above. They are original in motive and treatment, and also in melody, form and orchestral effects. They are all romantic in the strictest sense of the word.

The most popular of the three is "Der Freischuetz:" the other two, though they contain many beauties, and are acknowledged to be an advance, in some important respects, on the first, have never

CHAP. VIII.

Origin of romantic music

maintained their place on the stage, whereas the interest in " Der Freischuetz " seems to be permanent, at least in Germany. It is only natural that its popularity should be greater in Weber's native country than elsewhere, for it deals with themes peculiarly German, with popular German legends and superstitions, familiar alike to noble, burgher and peasant. The interest in the supernatural and the fantastic, which constitute so large a portion of the elements of this opera, is indeed universal ; but the mold in which these elements are cast is national. This applies both to the text and to Weber's beautiful and characteristic musical setting. The whole is the counterpart, in the domain of opera, of the Romantic literature then in the full vigor of its lusty youth. It was, of course, natural that the Romantic movement in music should come to its first development in the domain of opera, and that this epoch should be followed rather than preceded or accompanied by the period of romanticism in instrumental music; for, since this movement consisted essentially in the expression of romantic feelings in tones, the first suggestion of this would naturally come from a romantic text. Successful efforts to set such texts to appropriate music would naturally be followed by attempts to embody similar feelings in purely instrumental forms.

This was the actual course of musical history. So that, if Weber had written no pianoforte music, his creative activity in the field of Romantic Opera would have prepared the way for the purely romantic composers for the pianoforte. But the romantic ideas and feelings which had become the most powerful element in the intellectual and spiritual life of the time could not fail to produce a marked effect on all intellectual activity in whatsoever field.

We have seen that this romantic tendency was reproduced in Beethoven's instrumental works, and traces of it are also to be found in Weber's pianoforte compositions. In most of these, however, the romantic element appears at its worst and shallowest. It savors of sacrilege to mention Weber's concertos and sonatas in the same breath with the profoundly significant and essentially noble Beethoven works. Most of Weber's pianoforte pieces were written in his youth and early manhood, in the days when he had no feelings or purposes which could find noble expression in elevated music; when he was simply a brilliant, showy pianist, and when the expression of feeling in his playing so highly prized by his contemporaries was, in all probability, the shallow sentimentality of a weak-nerved, over-sensitive artist excited by gay or melancholy surroundings. At least, it is difficult to find much now in his pianoforte works which can account for the enthusiasm they excited in the first decade of the century. The influence of romantic ideas shows itself much less in the emotional content of them than in neglect or contempt of the principles of classical form, in a disregard of the intellectual requirements of the old ideals, and in a certain straining after effect and originality. These faults

The romantic in Weber's pianoforte works.

Shallowness of his early productions.

Ephemeral character of his pianoforte works.

are fatal, and Weber's pianoforte pieces are nowadays, for the most part, deservedly neglected.

The most prominent exception to the general rule is his "Invitation to Waltz," a master-piece in its originality of conception, its poetic beauty, its fire, vigor, refinement and delicacy, and in its force and truthfulness of characterization. This is, indeed, a romantic work, in the truest sense. It is not only far in advance of any other pianoforte piece by its author, but represents a certain phase of the Romantic movement more perfectly than any other work of the time. Its excellence has achieved for it a great and widespread popularity which bids fair to be lasting, either in its original form, in Berlioz's orchestral transcription, or in Carl Tausig's brilliant show-piece "arrangement" of it, a clever piece of virtuoso work which certainly has decided beauties of its own, though some of its most brilliant effects are obtained by the sacrifice of the finest poetic qualities of Weber's original conception. Besides this, the Rondo of his Sonata in C, known under the name "Perpetual Motion," still excites a good deal of interest, his "Concert Stueck" has not yet wholly disappeared from the repertoire of pianists, and a few other pieces are played more or less and are used, not always wisely, for teaching purposes.

The life of FRANZ PETER SCHUBERT, the greatest creative composer among Beethoven's contemporaries, was a short and uneventful one. He was the son of a poor parish schoolmaster, and was born in Vienna, January 31, 1797. He showed talent for music in his earliest childhood, and received lessons in singing and on the violin and the pianoforte. His teachers soon found that his intuitive perceptions had anticipated their instructions. In 1808 he was admitted as a singer into the choir of the Imperial Chapel. This appointment carried with it the right to an education in the "Stadt Convict," an institution where music was treated as an important branch of study. His evident ability soon brought him forward to the place of leader of the school orchestra, and here he studied the best music of the day, the symphonies of Haydn, Mozart and Beethoven, and became thoroughly familiar with the resources of the orchestra.

Becomes a choir singer in Vienna.

He soon felt the creative impulse, and began to compose numerous quartets, quintets, songs, pianoforte pieces, and finally a symphony. He tried his hand at opera also, but in this field he was never successful. His first symphony is dated October 18, 1813, and was performed by the school orchestra.

Soon after this his voice changed, and he had to leave the Imperial Chapel. He could have had the privilege of pursuing his school studies for some time longer, but his whole mind was devoted to music, and he was indifferent to all other intellectual pursuits. He did, indeed, become thoroughly acquainted with the whole range of German poetry, but he seems to have made it merely tributary to his musical creative impulses, and always remained exclusively a musician. When he left school after his five years of study he was forced to teach with

Leaves the choir and school and devotes his time exclusively to music.

his father in order to earn his bread. This occupation he found thoroughly distasteful, and the three years he passed in it were years of drudgery, only relieved by constant creative activity. He honestly and conscientiously fulfilled his duties as a teacher, but outside of these he devoted himself to composition with such zeal and industry that these years were among the most prolific of his life.

Nor, youth as he was, were all the compositions of this time unimportant. Two of his greatest songs, "The Erlking" and "The Wanderer," belong to the year 1816, and two symphonies, one in B flat and the "Tragic" in C minor, both of which have won a high reputation among those who have heard them. He discontinued his work as a school teacher during his twentieth year, and thenceforth he earned a scanty livelihood by teaching music and by the sale of his compositions. He made various applications for official posts as teacher or conductor, but never obtained one of them; he could find no publisher for the great majority of his works; very few of his songs were sung and only a small portion of his instrumental compositions were ever performed during his life time; he lived obscure and neglected and died in poverty, October 19, 1828.

Such is the brief record of the life of a composer, who, if he lacked some of the elements of greatness which go to make up a genius of the first rank, was, nevertheless, one of the most spontaneously creative minds known in human history. His imagination produced music as a tropical forest produces vegetation,—it was a soil of boundless fertility, crowded with germs which constantly sprang into marvellously luxuriant growth under the influence of tropical heat and moisture. The list of his works* is something enormous, and includes not only songs and short pieces, but masses and operas, nine symphonies, the last of which is one of the longest ever written.

The quality of these works are quite as remarkable as their quantity. The two best known symphonies, the ninth in C major and the Unfinished in B minor, are among the most beautiful, graceful, delicate and refined compositions ever written for the orchestra. The ideas are indeed not forceful, but neither are they weak; they lack the virility of Beethoven, but their essentially feminine quality is positive, not negative. If they have not the grandeur, the uplifting, inspiring power of Schubert's greatest contemporary, they have the enduring charm of grace, tenderness, delicacy, refined beauty and an emotional significance the complement of Beethoven's stormy moods. Beethoven climbed rugged mountain steeps, toiling painfully from rock to rock, with bleeding hands and lacerated knees, facing storm and hail, thunder and lightning, struggling indomitably against opposing powers of earth and air, his face turned ever upward to the heavenly beauty toward which he strove, whose beatific vision was at once his inspiration

*See H. F. Frost's biography of Schubert, Appendix. New York, Scribner & Welford.

CHAP. VIII.

His wealth of beautiful ideas.

His songs his most important contribution to musical history.

and his soul's peace. Schubert's imagination dwelt below in the luxuriant valley, full of flowers, of birds and of sunshine, in the repose of heaven's own light and air, singing and making melody with the spontaneity and ecstatic delight of a bird in a June meadow.

If he delights and surprises us by the fertility of his imagination and his wealth of beautiful and significant ideas, he charms us no less by the inexhaustible variety of his treatment of them. The C major symphony is indeed prolix, but its length is, as Schumann said, "heavenly;" no one not insensible to its subtle charm can wish for a moment that Schubert had applied the pruning knife to its beautiful luxuriance. There is not a spray or a twig we would willingly sacrifice.

But beautiful as are his symphonies, and great as was the treasure he bequeathed to the world in his instrumental works, his most important contribution to musical progress is to be found in his songs, of which he wrote some six hundred, and these more than anything else determine his place in musical history. His genius was essentially lyric and romantic;—romantic in that he loved to deal with romantic themes, and romantic also in his intuitive sense of fitness in characterization, and in his innate power of characteristic invention. What Weber did for the opera Schubert did for the song. He was the first creator of music adapted to express and intensify all the varying and contrasted phases of emotion suggested by the best lyric poems in German, and some of the best in English, literature. With him the song ceased to be merely a ballad form, corresponding in a merely general way with the emotional content of the words, and became a plastic, subtle, romantic medium for the most complete emotional expression. If in his instrumental compositions he loved to dwell on the gentle, the tender, dealing in quiet, pensive, reposeful moods, he could now and then deal with a vigorous, soul-stirring text with no lack of breadth, power or intensity, as, for example, in his "Erl-King." Nevertheless, these cases are comparatively few, and do not represent the natural and habitual cast of his mind. This is shown more characteristically in his "Dying Strains," and his "Maid of the Mill."

In the domain of pianoforte music, Schubert has left us a considerable body of compositions, beautiful, significant, characterized by qualities essentially romantic, and pointing distinctly toward the new development which was to follow him directly. In these works there are three points in which his romanticism reveals itself. 1. In the production of a large number of pieces which, though founded on the essential principles of form which had been once for all established, did not strictly conform to the plan of the sonata. The sonata form no longer fully met his needs as a medium of expression. With preceding composers the sonata had been the natural form in which their musical ideas took shape. Their strivings were in the direction of the completion of that form, and when they did not write whole sonatas they still cast their ideas in Rondo form, or in Dance form, both of which belonged to the sonata as components. Only rarely did they have something to say which could not find embodiment in these forms. The C minor Fantasia of Mozart is a conspicuous example of the exceptions to the rule.

Schubert's requirements in Form.

Beethoven's practice remained the same, except that he modified the sonata form itself to suit the requirements of his enlarged content. But Schubert, while he continued to write sonatas and symphonies which differed from classical models, so far as form was concerned, only in being more diffuse and prolix, seems to have had within him, probably without philosophizing at all on the subject, emotions he could not help expressing in music, which would hardly fit with exactness either the sonata or any of its component movements. So he wrote "Impromptus," "Momens Musicales," and "Fantasias," and wrote so many of them that instead of being a mere incident of his work as a composer they occupied an important part of his creative activity.

His lack of classical clearness and symmetry.

2. The second mark of his romanticism is the absence of the classical characteristics of compact, clearness of form, of concentration and symmetry. His sonatas are all rambling and diffuse. His imagination was extremely active, and not only constantly generated new ideas, but continually combined and contrasted them in an infinite variety of ways, rambling on and on till there seemed to be no

more limit to the ever-changing views than to those of a kaleidoscope. And every change revealed new beauties; every new light in which his ideas were set showed more and more clearly the loveliness of them; each new effect seemed more and more charming; and, as his fertility was inexhaustible and he seemed to be enamored of the grace and beauty of his conceptions and never to tire of turning them over and over, his productions were nearly always spun out to such lengths that he wholly lost sight of classical proportions. This enthusiasm, this fond dwelling upon his conceptions from the love of them, this giving himself up unreservedly to the pleasure of following his own spontaneous impulses, regardless of classical rules or of strict intellectual requirements of any sort, is an essentially romantic tendency.

Finally, the emotional content of his compositions is essentially romantic. We have already seen that he occupied himself less with considerations of form than did the purely classical writers. On the other hand, feeling comes more into the foreground; it is a more prominent and important factor. His sensibility is keenly alive, is open and sensitive to impressions; the range of feeling is wider, the emotional movements are more subtle, delicate, and refined; there is more complexity of feeling; emotions follow each other more rapidly, often contend with one another for supremacy; the contrasts are sharper and more sudden. Besides, these feelings are decidedly romantic in character, though they

His feelings were essentially romantic.

represent mainly the feminine side of the romantic type. These pieces are full of sentiment, of tenderness, of dreamy voluptuousness, occasionally interrupted by episodes of a more stirring and vigorous character. In short, all the phases of feeling to which Schubert gave expression in his songs, when he consciously sought to connect them with different scenes, situations and events, come equally to their embodiment in his instrumental works, and stamp them unmistakably with romantic characteristics.

In concluding this sketch of the Transition Period between the Classic and the Romantic, and of the three great composers whose genius and productive activity were chiefly instrumental in bringing about the inevitable change, a brief summing-up must suffice.

Be it remembered that the classical ideal was an *objective* one; that is, the composer's mind was occupied with an object outside of himself; with his ideal conception, and with the work of embodying it. Feeling, which is the innermost content of music, is *subjective;* is an internal experience. When the mind of the composer is mainly occupied with feeling, the intellectual side of his work becomes less prominent. The intellectual element becomes then only a means for the expression of the feeling.

In the Romantic writers, this predominance of feeling over the intellectual side of composition of content over form, is a prominent feature. The Romantic movement was the assertion of individualism in Art, of the importance of the private feelings of the composer and their right to truthful and vivid expression as against the classical tendency to thrust them into the background, to give them expression only incidentally and unconsciously, while the mental activity was taken up with the realization of an ideal conceived of as objective, as in a sense outside of and foreign to the composer. Be it remembered, further, that the change from the predominance of the classical to the Romantic ideal was not sudden ; it was a gradual development.

Order of development.

The first interest of men in music was that of sensuous gratification, the pleasure derived from sweet sounds, and from the excitement of rhythmical repetitions of sounds. Then came the intellectual interest and pleasure of arranging sounds in successions and combinations, the development of the technic of composition, of Counterpoint, Harmony and Form. This went on, hand in hand with the development of vocal and instrumental technics, and the invention and improvement of instruments. The clear perception of the relation of music to emotion is a later stage of development. It was felt at first dimly, more especially in purely instrumental music. No doubt, from the very beginning of song, the congruity or incongruity of words and music were instinctively felt ; this relation gradually impressed itself more and more on the minds of composers and connoisseurs, until finally the emotional significance of music forced itself into prominence, asserted its claims to recognition and deter-

Chap. VIII.

Weber's and Schubert's romanticism.

Beethoven the forerunner of both.

mined the downfall of the classical and the predominance of the Romantic ideal.

In Weber, we see this process carried to its completion in his operas, and exerting a marked influence on his pianoforte compositions. In Schubert, the same tendency reaches its culmination in his songs, with a similar effect on his instrumental writing. Beethoven is, in a way, the forerunner, although he is the contemporary of both. He was sixteen years older than Weber, and twenty-seven years older than Schubert; difference enough so that he prepared the way in which they advanced beyond him. In Beethoven's instrumental works, as well as in those of Schubert and Weber, feeling assumes great importance, becomes much more prominent than it had ever been in the older writers; but both Beethoven and Schubert seem to have been groping their way toward the Romantic ideal, led indeed by a sure instinct, but more or less blindly. Weber, in his "Invitation to Dance," seems for once to have reached a clearer and more definite conception of the goal to be reached than either of his great contemporaries.

PART THIRD.
THE ROMANTIC PERIOD,

CHAPTER IX.

THE ROMANTIC COMPOSERS FOR THE PIANOFORTE.

FELIX MENDELSSOHN-BARTHOLDY, 1809–1847.
FREDERIC CHOPIN, 1809–1849.
ROBERT SCHUMANN, 1810–1856.

FELIX MENDELSSOHN BARTHOLDY was born in Hamburg, February 3, 1809. His grandfather was the distinguished Jewish philosopher, Moses Mendelssohn. His father, Abraham, was a wealthy banker. His mother, Lea Salomon-Bartholdy, was also of Jewish blood, but was baptised with her husband into the Protestant communion, and the name of Bartholdy was added to the family name of Mendelssohn. Both the parents of Felix were persons of high character, superior intellectual abilities, refined feelings, cultivated tastes, and devoted much time and pains to the education of their children. Felix had two sisters, Fanny and Rebecca, and one brother, Paul. The family removed to Berlin before Felix was three years old, driven from Hamburg by the French occupation, and here they continued to reside *CHAP. IX. Mendelssohn. Character of the Mendelssohn family.*

Felix was taught by the best private tutors, studying, besides the ordinary branches, Greek, drawing, pianoforte, violin, harmony and composition. He also received thorough physical training, and was to *His early education.*

CHAP. IX.

Early productions.

the end of his life a proficient in all athletic exercises, a good swimmer, rider and dancer. His teacher in composition was Zelter, a strict, pedantic contrapuntist of the old school. Felix began to compose at twelve years of age, and his productive activity was incessant. He wrote songs, pianoforte pieces, chamber music, symphonies for a few instruments, operettas; and these were all played and sung at the musical parties periodically given in his father's house. Of course, few or none of these works of his apprentice period had permanent value. The work which signalized his majority as a composer was the overture to Shakspeare's "Midsummer Night's Dream," written in the summer of 1826, when he was seventeen years old. It was a most charming, delightful, original and characteristic work, of such excellence that he never surpassed it, even in his maturity.

"A Midsummer Night's Dream."

His general education was not neglected. He entered the university about this time, attended Hegel's lectures, among others, and distinguished himself by some admirable translations of Terence and Horace into German verse, in the meters of the originals. His production of music went on steadily, stimulated by intercourse with the best musicians, critics and connoisseurs of Berlin, and others who visited that city. The Mendelssohn home was a delightful and hospitable one, and few musicians came to the Prussian capital without visiting it. Felix, though sensitive and excitable, was of a thoroughly wholesome, happy disposition, and in his childhood and youth, no less than in his mature manhood, he charmed all who met him.

After the Midsummer Night's Dream overture the next important landmark in his progress was the overture to Goethe's "Calm Sea and Prosperous Voyage," in which his romanticism showed itself no less than in his earlier great work. In the Midsummer Night's Dream he had chosen a peculiarly romantic subject; had set himself the task of reproducing in tones the feelings aroused by the scenes of the play, and had been thoroughly successful. In this second overture he discarded the classic form, and made of the usual two movements two companion pieces intended to reproduce the impressions made on his feelings by the sea in calm and in storm. His success in this instance was no less marked. This overture was finished in 1829.

"The Meeres-stille" overture.

Another important event occurred in March of this year, the performance of Bach's great "Passion Music according to St. Matthew" for the first time since the death of its author. This was Mendelssohn's doing. He and Devrient, the actor, persuaded Zelter to allow its rehearsal by the Akademie of which he was director, Mendelssohn conducted, and the revival of this great work proved an immense popular success.

Revival of Bach's "Passion Music."

Abraham Mendelssohn now planned an extended tour for his son, with the object not only of improving his mind in a general way, but of enabling him to make friends, and find for himself a satisfactory place in which to settle and work. His first visit was

His travels

to London, when he played in public, produced some of his compositions, and made many friends. He was cordially received by the public, and found London so congenial that he always felt a warm affection for the place and people, returning there nine different times in the course of his life. He traveled in England and Scotland, and received deep and lasting impressions from some of the scenery. The "Scotch" symphony and the "Hebrides Overture" are attempts to reproduce these impressions in tones. The latter is due to the effect produced on his feelings by a visit to Fingal's cave. But neither of these pieces was written at the time; some of the principal motives occurred to him there, but the impressions lay in his mind for a long time before they matured and took musical shape. His first great symphony was the "Reformation Symphony," written after his return from England, in the winter of 1829-30, for the tercentenary festival of the Augsburg Confession.

In May, 1830, he began a long tour on the continent, through Germany, Switzerland, Austria, Italy, France, and at last to London again. It was July, 1832, before he again reached Berlin. These two years were a delightful time, and a period of growth and improvement. Mendelssohn enjoyed the scenery, the society of artists and literary men, sketched a great deal, played much in public, in short, enjoyed thoroughly and with hearty zest whatever was enjoyable in his travels, but he did not neglect composition. During this time he wrote for the pianoforte the G minor concerto, the capriccio in B minor, the first book of the Songs without Words, and some other things. His correspondence was extensive, and his letters are the most charming productions imaginable, and give us, better than anything else can, an insight into the personal fascination he exercised on all who came in contact with him.

The "Italian Symphony" was written at Berlin in the winter of 1832-3. In May of the latter year he conducted the Lower Rhine Festival at Duesseldorf with great success, and this resulted in a three years' engagement as director of music there, involving his responsibility for all the town music in the churches, the concerts and the theater. From this last he soon withdrew, influencing the opera selections and performances only indirectly. He composed steadily, writing many of his smaller pieces and beginning his oratorio of St. Paul in March, 1834.

In October, 1835, he accepted the post of conductor of the Gewandhaus concerts in Leipzig, and here he spent nearly all the remainder of his life. He did indeed accept temporarily an appointment as Kapellmeister to the King of Prussia, and as head of a new Academy of Music in Berlin, and even removed there, but unendurable irritation and worry came of his relations with the Prussian court; his heart was in Leipzig, he soon returned there, and there he lived and died. His connection with Berlin continued in part after he left the city. He paid repeated visits to London, conducted festivals in Germany, etc., but his principal work was done in conducting the Gewandhaus concerts, in founding and directing the Leipzig Conservatory (in 1843), and in composition. St Paul was finished in 1836, and met with immediate success.

In March, 1837, he was married at Frankfort to Cecile Jeanrenaud, daughter of a Protestant pastor there. The union was an extremely fortunate one, and conduced greatly to his happiness and usefulness. But this useful, happy life was cut prematurely short. He was an indefatigable worker. Incessant labor, combined with his excitable nervous temperament, which gave intensity to all emotional experiences, whether pleasurable or painful, and made them a serious drain upon his vitality, wore him out at the age of thirty-eight. The finishing stroke was given by the strain of producing his great oratorio "Elijah," written for the Birmingham Festival of August 25, 1846, at which he himself conducted. He never recovered from the prostration which this occasioned. Although he continued to work, he gradually became weaker, suffered from severe pains in the head, and finally died, November 4, 1847. The details of his life are so easily accessible that the foregoing brief sketch may suffice for this place.*

*See Lampadius' " Life of Mendelssohn," " The Mendelssohn Family," by S. Hensel, son of Felix's sister Fanny, Devrient's " Recollections of Mendelssohn," Hiller's " Letters and Recollections of Mendelssohn, Carl Mendelssohn's " Goethe and Mendelssohn, ' Benedict's " A sketch of the Life and Works of the late Felix Mendelssohn-Bartholdy, ' two volumes of

The great works here referred to are by no means all he produced, but they are perhaps the most important and characteristic. The music to Goethe's "Walpurgis Night" ought, however, to be mentioned as especially displaying his romantic tendencies. The nature of the subject was such that any music appropriate to it must necessarily have been romantic.

His pianoforte music, of which he wrote a large quantity, has, much of it, an emotional content closely analagous to that of the "Midsummer Night's Dream" overture and the rest of his compositions for orchestra. Such, for example, are the "Rondo Capriccioso" in E minor, op. 14, the "Capriccio" in B minor, the "Andante Cantabile and Presto Agitato," the "Serenade and Allegro giojoso," and many of his "Songs Without Words." These latter are thoroughly characteristic of him, original in form and in content, though many of them, as well as some of his other compositions, fall below the significance of the best, as was, of course, inevitable. Very few of these pieces have any title to indicate the scenes or persons to whose influence the emotions embodied in the music were due, but it is known that he was in the habit of trying to reproduce in tones the emotional impressions received from his surroundings. Of course, many of these impressions were not profound,—he did

His romantic tendencies as shown in "The Walpurgis Night" music.

Content of his pianoforte music.

his letters, one " From Italy to Switzerland," and the other " From 1833 to 1847," and an excellent article in Grove's " Dictionary of Music and Musicians." This list is by no means exhaustive.

HISTORY OF PIANOFORTE MUSIC.

CHAP IX.

Special characterization of his music.

not attempt to restrict his musical utterances to his most important feelings, but often sought to embody in tones a content little removed from elegant commonplace. Accordingly much of his music is not at all remarkable for its profound emotional significance. But it is always genuine, graceful, refined, elegant, and everywhere displays the hand of a consummate master.

How his romanticism appeared in the forms he chose.

Special attention ought to be called to the evidences of Mendelssohn's romanticism displayed in the forms assumed by his most characteristic utterances. He not only deliberately sought to emphasize the expression of feeling as the goal of his efforts in composition, but when he succeeded in reproducing his emotions in tones, the completed products were almost always departures from the classical models. The pieces on which his reputation as a pianoforte composer depend are not sonatas, perhaps not even his concertos, but "Capriccios," "Fantasias," and "Songs without Words."

His forms were always finished and clear.

But it would be a serious misapprehension to suppose that his forms were often, or indeed ever crude, imperfect, or lacking in clearness or finish. Romanticist as he undoubtedly was, the romantic element represented only one side of his character. The purest of classicists could not have written with more perfect clearness of outline, absolute precision of detail, and perfection of finish. There is nothing obscure or foggy,—there are no half utterances, no stammering or failure. What he had to say he expressed with the utmost precision and certainty, with a clearness and finish above criticism.

Indeed, it may fairly be questioned whether the very lucidity and polish of his style does not often detract from the effectiveness of his pieces. They are expressive rather than suggestive, and expressive, too, of a content not always profound enough to be interesting, still less inspiring. If we could feel, as we often do with Schumann, that much is left unsaid, that the comparatively insignificant content here expressed with such consummate grace and elegance, had evident relation to more important things not far off, their attraction would be much enhanced. The very completeness with which Mendelssohn gave utterance to so many graceful insipidities was the cause of a strong reaction against his influence and tendencies not many years after his death. It is not uncommon, even now, to hear his music referred to somewhat sneeringly as "very gentlemanly music," while his fellow romanticists are exalted at his expense. The amount of justice in this has perhaps already been sufficiently indicated.

Whatever may be the permanent significance or influence of Mendelssohn's best work, he was, as man, musician, conductor, pianist, organist and composer, one of the most powerful influences in molding the musical thought and shaping the musical tendencies of the second and third quarters of this century; he was a musician of the highest technical attainments, the broadest and most enlight-

Less suggestive than Schumann

Estimate of his character and work.

ened culture, a consummate master of form, an original inventor in the domain of melody and harmony, and in his own peculiar field of romantic emotional expression he was unapproached. This is probably the most that can be said for his pianoforte music

His works perfect in their way.

Measured by the standard of form, finish, musicianship, grace, elegance, refinement, polish, delicacy, beauty, he is surpassed by few or none. He must be credited, too, with genuine originality and creative power. But measured by the standard of nobility, elevation and profound significance of emotional content, the best of his pianoforte works will poorly bear comparison with the greatest utterances of Beethoven, though they may well be placed beside the finest of Schubert's works, and are greatly superior to almost everything of Weber.

Content of his oratorios.

His "St. Paul" and "Elijah" stand on a higher emotional plane. They contain noble passages, and sublime climaxes, and "Elijah" has scenes of immense dramatic force. That these works have great and positive merits and high significance is certainly undeniable. The question of their claims to immortality must be left to future generations for settlement. But there can be no question as to the beneficent influence they have already exerted. Their author certainly had a place and mission of his own in the world; he most admirably filled the one and accomplished the other.

F. F. Chopin.

FRANÇOIS FREDERIC CHOPIN was born in Zelazowa Wola, a village near Warsaw, March 1, 1809. His father, Nicholas Chopin, was a Frenchman from Lorraine, who had settled in Warsaw when a young man, and was engaged in teaching the French language, as a professor in the Lyceum, an institution corresponding in a general way to our colleges. He also taught in various Government schools, military and other, and was, besides, a private teacher, receiving young men of family into his household.

Frederic's mother was a Polish lady, Justine Kryzanowska. There were three daughters, one of whom died young, of consumption; but Frederic was the only son. He seems to have taken his character mainly from his mother, his traits being decidedly more Polish than French, and he always counted himself a Pole. Indeed, his father had thoroughly identified himself with his adopted country, and the political events of the times were so impressive, the misfortunes of Poland were so great and fell with such crushing force upon all residents of Poland that patriotic feeling was not only excited to the highest pitch, but every Pole was forced to feel the humiliation and sorrow of grinding tyranny and oppression. The Poles were proud, sensitive, excitable, and felt the sting of their national degradation as keenly as human beings could feel. Besides this, after the partition of 1772, almost every Pole, however noble or distinguished, was exposed to personal insult and abuse. Polish hearts, Chopin's among the rest, were mainly occupied with the feelings called forth by their national calamities. In this we may find the key to the emotional content of many of his compositions, and thus account for much in them which has always impressed connoisseurs as being somewhat morbid.

His character and manners.

Young Chopin was naturally refined, and was brought up from earliest childhood in intimate association with the best society of the Polish capital. His manners were graceful and winning; while at the same time he was reserved; much more so than was evident on the surface of his behavior. His constitution was not robust, and he had a delicate and susceptible nervous organization, but was, nevertheless, sound and healthy,—was, indeed, never ill in his life until he contracted consumption in Paris, at about the age of thirty.*

His education.

His father gave him a liberal education at the Lyceum, and put him into the hands of two excellent music teachers, Albert Zywny, who was his only teacher in piano-playing and who made him a pianist of the first rank before he was twenty, and Joseph Elsner, a sound and excellent German musician, who taught him Harmony, Counterpoint and Composition.

Early manifestations of genius.

The boy's genius and originality soon began to be manifest, both in improvisation and in formal composition. He was very fond of the Polish national folk-songs and dances, and seizing upon these strange melodies, with their peculiar rhythms,

---

*Liszt's book on Chopin is a magazine of misinformation on this and numerous other points, though it contains much valuable suggestion and throws a great deal of light on Chopin's character and works to those who can discriminate the errors from the truth. See article in Grove's "Dictionary of Music and Musicians."

he supplied them with original harmonies of his own, invented cadences peculiar to himself and unique in the history of music, and invested them with a poetic charm and significance which raised them at once to high artistic rank. His imagination was vivid, subtle and powerful, and being kindled by the peculiar circumstances in his surroundings, to which he was most susceptible, he began almost in childhood to express the national feelings in musical productions of the most ideally poetic character. He was extremely modest and retiring, but his gifts could not be concealed, and his playing was eagerly sought for and listened to with delight by the best connoisseurs of Warsaw. His first public performance was in 1818, when he was nine years of age. On this occasion he played a concerto by Gyrowetz, and was well received, but so far was he from being vain of his success as a player, that when his mother asked him about it he cried, "O mamma, everybody was looking at my new collar!"

When he was eighteen years old his father determined to send him to Berlin, in order that he might meet musicians, hear more music than could be heard in Warsaw, and under better conditions than prevailed there, and widen his experience generally. Accordingly, to Berlin went the boy, in company with his father's friend, Professor Jarocki. He heard a great deal, keenly observed all that was to be seen and heard, received numerous impressions which were of benefit to him, but neither played nor

Chap. IX.

First playing in public.

Journey to Berlin.

showed his compositions. He had opportunities to meet Mendelssohn, Spontini and Zelter, but was too modest to avail himself of them. "I did not think it becoming," he writes to one of his young friends, "to introduce myself to these gentlemen."*

This journey taught him much and stimulated him more. He returned to Warsaw and worked nearly two years with redoubled zeal and industry. At length, in July, 1829, his father sent him away again, this time to Vienna, and urged upon him the importance of not only making the acquaintance of the best musicians of the great musical capital, but also of making himself known by playing in public.

The young man did both. He carried letters of introduction to some of the most intelligent and influential persons in the city; they at once perceived his great gifts, though he himself was modestly unconscious of them and "wondered what they found to admire in him," and all, musicians and laymen alike, pressed him to play in public. He appeared in two concerts. In the first he played his variations on "La ci darem," op. 2, and improvised on two themes, one from "La Dame Blanche," and one a Polish theme. In the second he played his "Krakowiak," op. 14, repeating the variations, by request. Both his playing and his music aroused great enthusiasm. The admiration was nearly universal, and Chopin left Vienna, after a short stay,

---

*See " Friedrich Chopin, Sein Leben, Seine Werke und Briefe," von Moritz Karasowski, Vol. 1, p. 57. This is the one authentic biography of Chopin, and it is to be hoped that it may shortly be translated into English.

amidst flattering plaudits. He went home by a roundabout way, through Prague and Dresden, reached Warsaw about the first of September, and again settled down to work.

CHAP. IX.

His Vienna experience, short as it was, did much to mature his character and talent. The day after his first concert, an event of great importance to him, he wrote to his parents a very modest letter, giving a full account of the whole affair, and toward the end wrote, "I am now at least four years older in knowledge and experience."* The enthusiastic praise he received from the best artists and connoisseurs awakened his courage and gave him confidence in his own powers, while it stimulated him to the exercise of them.

Effect of his Vienna experience on his development.

Another event was now a powerful stimulus to production; he had become passionately enamored of Constantia Gladkowska, a young lyric actress at the Warsaw theatre. It was the pure, elevated first love of a high-minded, refined artist, and much came of it in the way of composition. His emotions, powerfully excited by this passion, as well as by the events of his visit to Vienna, sought musical expression, and the next year was a very productive one, the most important works being the Etudes, op. 10, and his two concertos, in E minor and in F minor. In a letter to one of his very few intimate friends, dated October 3, 1829, he speaks of being invited to Berlin by the Prince and Princess Radziwill, but says he has begun so many works that he thinks it

His first love affair.

His two concertos and the Etudes, op. 10.

*See Karasowski, Vol. 1, p. 79.

would be wiser to remain in Warsaw. In the next paragraph of the same letter he confides to his friend that he has found his ideal, but does not mention the name of the young lady; says he idolizes her, but has never yet spoken with her. He says also that the thought of her inspired him in the composition of the Adagio of his new concerto, and of a waltz* he had just written. His concerto in F minor, afterwards published as op. 21, was finished, and Chopin played it in two concerts in the Warsaw theatre in March, 1830. His success with the public was immense, and gave him still further encouragement.

First public performance of the E minor concerto.

The E minor concerto, published as op. 11, was finished in August, and on the eleventh of October he played it in concert with the same success which had hitherto attended his public performances. The critics praised him without stint, and his countrymen were proud of him as an artist who did honor to the Polish nation.

Technical difficulties of the concertos.

They had indeed abundant reason for their pride. If he had accomplished nothing more than the mere mastery of the technical difficulties of these two concertos, he would have ranked as one of the greatest virtuosos who had appeared up to this time. In

*See Karasowski, Vol. 1, p. 108. A foot note informs us that the E minor concerto is the one referred to, and this statement is repeated on page 123. But the evidence furnished by Karasowski is conclusive that the F minor concerto was played in public before the first and last movements of the one in E minor were written. Possibly the Adagio of the latter was written before the other movements, and while he was at work on the former. But Karasowski offers us no evidence whatever in support of his statement.

fact, these difficulties were not only very great, but they were of so peculiar a kind as to form an epoch in the history of pianoforte technics, and there was hardly anybody at that time, except Chopin himself and his great contemporary, Liszt, who could have played them. Pianists had to accustom themselves to the new manner before they could find themselves at home in it. But to have invented these new figures and combinations was a much greater feat.

When we consider the artistic significance of these works, the depth, fullness and variety of their emotional content, the force of contrast, the vigor, subtlety and vividness of imagination, the richness of harmony and modulation, the beauty of the melodies, the perfection of form, the ease and power with which the intellectual elements are controlled, the sure intuition by which the musical means are adapted to the requirements of expression, the refinement which pervades the whole, we must admit that in this young man of twenty-one we have before us one of the most original creators yet known, of whom not only Poland but the whole world might justly be proud.

With these two concertos Chopin left his home for Vienna, November 2, 1830.* He never returned

---

*The statement in Mr. Edward Dannreuther's admirable, though brief article on Chopin, in Grove's "Dictionary of Music and Musicians," that Chopin was only *nineteen* at this time, is a singular slip on the part of a usually careful writer. The evidence in Karasowski's book, to which Mr. Dannreuther refers, though he carelessly overlooked the facts, is conclusive.

to Warsaw, and with this departure closed the epoch of his youth. His friends accompanied him a short distance on his way, and at a banquet in a neighboring village presented him with a silver cup filled to the brim with Polish soil, solemnly adjuring him never to forget friends and fatherland. There was no need of the exhortation; Chopin was true and faithful, and loved his country and his home with ardent passion. This cup and its contents he kept religiously to the end of his life, and this Polish earth was, at his own request, strewn on his coffin at his burial.

Second visit to Vienna, 1830.

He traveled to Vienna by way of Breslau, Dresden and Prague, but he found the conditions there much less favorable for him than on his former visit. Many of his old friends were absent, and various circumstances conspired to prevent his giving concerts as he had intended, although he finally gave a single one to a small audience, not long before his departure.

The uprising at Warsaw.

Among these unfavorable circumstances was the Polish uprising of November 29th, 1830. The Austrian government and nobility became suspicious of all Poles and very much disinclined to favor them in any way, and Chopin's sympathies were so much with his oppressed and desperate countrymen that only the urgent representations of his father as to his unfitness for military duty kept him from returning at once to Warsaw to join his young friends in the ranks of the insurgents. Thus Vienna was no longer the pleasant place he had found it a year before, and he determined to go to Paris. But Paris was the headquarters of insurrection. It was the success of the July Revolution in Paris which had given hope to the Poles and been the occasion of the present outbreak. A Pole seeking a passport for Paris was a suspicious character, and Chopin's application was refused. He then applied for a passport for England, via Paris, and after considerable delay received permission to go as far as Munich on his way. He reached the Bavarian capital, July 20, 1831, remained there a few weeks, made the acquaintance of the best artists there, and, at their urgent request, played his E minor concerto in one of the concerts of the Philharmonic Society. His playing as well as his composition met with a reception which went far to compensate him for his disappointments in Vienna. But a severe blow was in store for him. In Stuttgart he received the news of the taking of Warsaw by the Russians, and was naturally filled with anxiety and grief. In this frame of mind he gave vent to his feelings in the passionate, fiery Etude in C minor, op. 10, No. 12, sometimes called the "Revolution Etude," a composition every way worthy of its author and of the occasion which called it forth.

He arrived in Paris toward the end of September, and there he remained, barring occasional journeys, for the rest of his life. The fate of his native country drove the greater part of the noble and intelligent among his countrymen into exile; many

CHAP. IX.

Discouragements.

Kalkbrenner.

Kalkbrenner's reception of him.

of them settled in Paris, and Chopin was much more at home there than he could possibly have been in Warsaw. So, after a while, he became a naturalized French citizen, and used to refer jokingly to his Vienna passport "to London, via Paris," saying that he was only on his way to England.

But the beginning of his life in Paris was far from encouraging. He was too modest to put himself forward by giving concerts, or in any other way, and he was wholly unknown. Success in Vienna, or indeed anywhere in Europe, did not involve success in Paris or the slightest reputation in that vainglorious metropolis. Chopin imagined himself in need of further instruction and bethought him of taking lessons of Kalkbrenner, at that time the most fashionable teacher in Paris, a robust, healthy artisan of a player, without a particle of genius in his composition, whose vigorous style of playing, combined with his really high technical attainments, made him pass for the greatest virtuoso in Europe.

This man, now wholly forgotten, the whole list of whose compositions is not worth the ink it would take to print a Chopin mazurka, had then such a reputation that Chopin, already an artist whose shoes Kalkbrenner was not worthy to loose, actually went to him and began negotiations for lessons. Kalkbrenner heard him play, saw at once what an increase of reputation such a pupil would give him, began to pick flaws in his technic, assured him that his playing did not conform to classical rules and needed a great deal of overhauling, and finished by informing him that he would need three years to train him properly, and would accept him as a pupil if he would agree to remain with him that length of time.

Chopin was very modest indeed, but he had sufficient knowledge of his own powers and attainments to be surprised at this proposal; perhaps, too, a suspicion that to become a second Kalkbrenner was not the high calling to which he was chosen, began to dawn upon him before the interview was over; at any rate, he hesitated and determined to ask advice of his father and of his former excellent teacher, Elsner, before deciding the matter. Elsner wrote him a wise and cautious letter, in which, without advising him directly what he should do, he laid down the principles which ought to guide his decision. He suggested plainly enough that Chopin ought to give his own genius a chance to develop naturally in its own way, and not allow any blind Philistine to cramp it by pseudo-classical restrictions, or distort it by crowding it into a mould for which nature never intended it, that ·his gifts as a a composer were of far more permanent importance than his piano-playing, and that three years devoted to acquiring the Kalkbrenner virtuosity was very much more time than he could afford to give to any such purpose. Meanwhile, Chopin had had several more interviews with the distinguished Parisian virtuoso, had played for him a good deal, had obtained from him the admission that he hardly needed three years of training in order to be-

CHAP. IX.

come a great pianist, and had come to much the same conclusions as those hinted at in his old teacher's guarded letter.

It had become clear to him that the Kalkbrenner virtuosity was no model for him, that on no account could he nor would he copy any such example; that even the truly classical field, whatever its richness and fertility, was not his field; still less could he see any way of producing anything from the little barren, stony patch so assiduously cultivated by the Parisian pianists and composers in total unconsciousness of its sterility. In short, the young man had been making the comparisons forced upon his attention and had fairly begun to be conscious of his own powers. He saw that his productions were wholly different, both in form and in content, from what he saw around him. He could not help believing in the validity of the principles which guided him and of the inward forces which strove in him for outward manifestation, nor could he longer conceal from himself that the legitimate outcome of these forces and principles must be to create a new epoch in the history of musical Art. And so, with strengthened courage and impulse, with firm and high purpose, he addressed himself eagerly and hopefully to the special and peculiar work, which he now clearly saw it had been given him to do. All this he boldly, but still modestly, announces to Elsner in his reply to his teacher's fatherly letter: he says decidedly that whatever study he now does will be pursued with a view to enabling

He acquires a real perception of his own powers.

him to stand more firmly on his own feet, gratefully acknowledges Elsner's wise and fatherly counsel, and dutifully hopes his kind friend will not withhold his approval and blessing.

But what to do for a living? His acquaintances, outside of a small circle of artists and a larger one of his impoverished refugee countrymen, were few; he could not at once sell his compositions; he had no pupils. His artist friends, Kalkbrenner among them, encouraged him to give a concert and helped him with the necessary arrangements, but many hindrances stood in the way, and when he at last gave it, in February, 1832, hardly anybody went except the more wealthy of his own countrymen, and the concert did not pay expenses. Chopin, always easily depressed, was very much discouraged. He conceived the idea of going to America, and wrote his parents, beseeching them to give their consent to his plan. Karasowski has some pertinent remarks as to the intolerable position in which such a sensitive, retiring, aristocratic artist would have found himself in practical, unpoetic, democratic America, if he had been unwise enough to settle here in 1832! Fifty years have made a wonderful change.

But Chopin's parents knew better. They insisted that he should either remain in Paris or return to Warsaw, and in spite of the numerous attractions of the French capital, his discouragements there combined with his home sickness to decide him to brave the displeasure of the Russian Government and go home. His friends in Paris, Liszt among others, in vain tried to dissuade him; his trunk was already packed when he happened to meet Prince Radiwill in the street, told him of his intention and bade him good-bye. The Prince pressed him to go with him that evening to a reception at Baron Rothschild's. Chopin consented, and that evening proved the turning point in his career. His hostess invited him to play; he was excited and inspired by his surroundings; played and improvised in a way that drew forth universal enthusiasm and applause from the company, and found himself at once on the road to fame and fortune. Before he left the house he had numerous applications to give lessons in the best families of Paris. He gave up his plan of leaving, and henceforth depended on his earnings for a livelihood. There was not the slightest difficulty about it; he at once became the fashion, grew more and more popular among the wealthy and cultivated Parisians, turned the heads of the beautiful women in the French metropolis, his compositions were eagerly bought as fast as they were published, and as pianist, teacher and composer he was, to the day of his death, the idol of society.

As a concert player, however, he was comparatively unsuccessful. His playing was fine, delicate, tender; he loved to play a piano with a soft, delicate tone, and his proper place was in a drawing-room, not a large theatre or concert-hall. This he discovered, to his mortification, at his second concert in Paris, where he failed to make any effect with the great audience in the vast auditorium of the Italian Opera. Henceforth public playing became distasteful to him; he left it to his friend Liszt who, as he said, "could storm and deafen the public into surrender," and played almost exclusively in small parties of connoisseurs, where, under the influence of sympathetic auditors, especially ladies, his finest artistic qualities showed themselves.

Thus Chopin all at once found himself floating on the top wave of prosperity But there was trouble in store for the young artist. In 1832, Constantia Gladkowska was married in Warsaw. Chopin's letters to his friend,* Johannes Matuszynski, prove that his love for her was pure, deep and passionate. This love he had never confided to his parents, and there had been no acknowledged engagement, but Constantia had at least so far encouraged him that, on his departure from Warsaw, she gave him a ring as a token of affection. Her marriage must have been a terrible disappointment to him, and a great mortification as well, though no record of his feelings on this subject exists. But Chopin was young, popular, had only too much to distract his thoughts, and time heals even severe hurts.

In his next love affair he was equally unfortunate, and even more so, so far as the wound to his self-love was concerned. In 1836 he was betrothed to a young and beautiful countrywoman of his, and he

CHAP. IX.

Love disappointments.

A second misfortune in love.

---

* See Karasowski, Vol. I, chap. X.

and all his friends were rejoicing in the near prospect of a happy marriage, when the young lady suddenly decided to accept a count for her husband, and broke with her artist-lover without warning or ceremony. It was a cruel humiliation, and no human being could have felt its sting more keenly or deeply than did Chopin. It rankled terribly, the more that he was not at all demonstrative by nature. He brooded over his feelings in secret, grew even more reserved and melancholy than usual, and finally became morbid and almost desperate.

In this mood he made the acquaintance of a most remarkable woman, who was henceforth to exercise a controlling power in his life.

His connection with George Sand. Her character.

Mme. Aurora Dudevant, known in literature under her pseudonym of "George Sand," was a woman of genius, and already held a commanding position in the literary world. The vigor and fire of her imagination, combined with the force, refinement and artistic finish of her style, had made her known as a consummate literary artist, and had given her a high place in the world's estimation, and especially in the coterie of writers, painters, musicians, artists and distinguished amateurs, of which Chopin was by no means the least important member. In personal character Mme. Sand was peculiar. She was powerful, almost masculine in her mental and bodily traits. She was passionate, but not coarse ; religious, without accepting any of the current theological dogmas ; moral in her way, but with a moral sense which most right thinking people would consider perverted, for she held opinions the legitimate outcome of which would be to dissolve the bonds of society. She was, in short, a free-lover in belief and practice, was separated from her husband, and supported herself and her two children by her pen. Her principles and conduct were no bar to her admission into a society where dullness was the greatest of crimes, and wit, not to say genius, atoned for many moral delinquencies, provided they were covered with a veil of decorum.

From any introduction to this woman Chopin had shrunk. He knew her books, admired her genius, but felt, nevertheless, a strong prejudice against her, and a desire to avoid her. Hitherto he had been successful in doing so, but just at the crisis of his second love affair she was presented to him one evening at a reception, fell violently in love with him, flattered him by her praise and attention, succeeded in fascinating him, and soon inspired him with a strong feeling of affection. He went at length to live at her house, and continued his intimate relations with her until 1847, when she tired of him, grew cool, and showed so plainly that she had outlived her passion that Chopin, already nearly dead with consumption, withdrew from her house and left her to her own devices. But his attachment to her had become his strongest passion, and the rupture with her proved fatal to him.

His illness had been a lingering one. It began with a severe attack of bronchitis in 1837. He sought relief in a Southern climate, spent the winter of

Chopin's prejudice against her.

Is captured by her.

His lingering illness.

1837-8 with Mme. Sand in the island of Majorca, and appeared to grow better after his return. But consumption began very soon, and was aggravated by late hours and the excitement of Parisian society. Its progress was slow but sure. For a long time before he left Mme. Sand's house he gave his lessons lying on a sofa, occasionally rising for a moment to give an example or make some necessary correction. During his illness, too, he became very irritable and his pupils had often to grant the pardon which he always asked for breaches of a courtesy which had never failed during the earlier portion of his life. Two years he lingered on after the last of his social disappointments and then he died, surrounded and mourned by his friends and pupils, October 17, 1849.

The preludes of a morbid character.

The last twelve years of his life require no detailed mention here. The record would be a monotonous one. His character had already been formed, and many of his greatest productions had seen the light before this time. The Preludes, or most of them, were written during his winter in Majorca, and many of them show traces of his morbid mental condition. He was suffering from his disorder; the winter was unusually cold and stormy; he was exceedingly nervous and a prey to hypochondriacal fancies, which at times bordered on insanity. This condition of mind was not permanent, but often recurred during the last years of his life, as his disease grew upon him and his sorrows increased ; and the compositions of these years often reflect his delirious mental condition. It is difficult to decide, however, just what compositions are to be assigned to this period of his life. The opus numbers are no guide; they only indicate the order of publication, not of composition, and many of the works published after his death were written in very early life.

The order of composition is approximately as follows: From op. 1 to op. 15, inclusive, were written before he went to Paris; so was the Concerto, op. 21, which was composed before the other; from op. 16 to op. 52, fall between 1832 and 1843; from op. 53 to op. 65, belong to the years 1843 to 1847. The works numbered from op. 66 onward are all posthumous, and with the single exception of the Fantasie-Impromptu, op. 66, are comparatively insignificant pieces, which Chopin himself intended to destroy.*

Of all his works, none are characterized by more beauty, freshness, originality, or vigor than his Concerto in E minor, op. 11. Of the works written in Paris before 1843, when his disease began to be serious, those most original in form are the Ballads, Scherzos and Impromptus. Some of the Nocturnes, Mazurkas and Polonaises are, however, equally characteristic and significant as regards their content, and extremely original in melody, harmony, cadences,

*There are two admirable complete editions of Chopin's works, one or both of which ought to be in the hands of every student. One edited by Carl Klindworth, and published by Bote & Bock, in Berlin, in three volumes, at $3.00 each, and one edited by Hermann Scholtz, and published by C. F. Peters, in three volumes, in Leipzig, at $1.75 each, or $5.00 for the complete edition.

Chap. IX.

Approximate order of his compositions.

His works.

figures and phraseology. The most important compositions after this period were the splendid and imposing Polonaise in A flat, op. 53, the Polonaise-Fantasie, op. 61, and the beautiful Berceuse, op. 57. But while there are degrees of excellence in his works, there is almost nothing from Chopin's pen which is not beautiful, poetic, significant, full of the real inspiration of true genius, the expression of the innermost life of a born artist, a passionate lover and worshipper of the Beautiful, serving his beloved Art and its ideal aims with unswerving and conscientious devotion.

As regards the emotional content of these works, perhaps little need be added to what has already been said. Chopin's emotional life was determined first of all by his inherited traits, mostly Polish, then by the political disasters which befell his country, and the consequent personal misfortunes of his friends and countrymen, and lastly, by his intellectual life and his social relations. His life in Paris was an exciting one, in spite of his comparative seclusion from the public. He was in daily intercourse with the most intellectual men and women of Parisian society,—artists, authors, wits, such persons as Heinrich Heine, Eugene Delacroix, Ary Scheffer, Franz Liszt, Mme. George Sand. His evenings were passed in the salons of beautiful, intelligent, aristocratic ladies, whose subtle charms attracted this select company of congenial spirits; and there Art, Literature and the higher life of intelligence were supreme. In this circle the noblest among

Chopin's countrymen found place, and in him they found a most ardent sympathizer with all their past sorrows, the woes of their present exile and their patriotic hopes and aspirations.

There is a certain heroic vein in many of his compositions which comes of his glowing patriotism, notably in his Polonaises, which are among the most characteristically national of his productions. But this heroism is, after all, a very different quality from that which in Beethoven we call by the same name. It lacks the ethical element, and it never suggests religious elevation. The heroic feelings expressed in these works savor more of pride of birth, of military ardor, of national humiliation, of the outraged self-love of a people, once celebrated for glorious military achievements but now downtrodden and oppressed, than of the moral indignation of the reformer, the struggle with temptation and with outward hindrance to the higher life, the striving after the highest ideals in character. Not that Chopin is ignoble, or immoral, or even irreligious; not at all. He was brought up a strict Catholic, and his early religious training, not unmixed with puerile superstition, was the ground on which his whole character was based. He was highminded, his whole mental activity was permeated with a fine moral sense, with refinement and high-bred courtesy. He was a man of the world in the best and highest sense, but still a man of the world. His interests are human interests; his relations human relations; his joys and sorrows grow out of

Chap. IX.

Heroic vein in his Polonaises.

The ethical element wanting.

His feeling mostly secular.

his social surroundings, and when bitter disappointment overtakes him his consolations are to be found in his relations to his fellows and in his beloved Art. His highest mental resource seems to be the love of the Beautiful and the power to create beautiful forms adapted to his need of emotional expression.

He perfectly expresses the feelings of the society in which he lived.

To Chopin we go then for perfect expression of the emotions engendered in a high-bred exclusive, intellectual society, as well as of those peculiar to himself and his nation, and for perfect embodiment of beautiful conceptions in highly original forms; not for moral inspiration or religious uplifting. The "religious passion and elevation" and the "widening of men's moral horizon" justly ascribed to Beethoven are not to be found in Chopin. By so much is the Polish composer inferior, in that the content of his greatest works is on a lower emotional plane than that occupied by the noblest utterances of his great predecessor.

Chopin's originality equal to any one's.

In originality and power of conception, in invention, in mastery of his musical material he is inferior to no one. What he had to say was his own, it was great and beautiful, and he said it in a manner above criticism; but it was not the highest and noblest thing yet said in the language of the pianoforte.

R. Schumann.

ROBERT SCHUMANN was born in Zwickau, then an insignificant mining town in Saxony, June 8, 1810. He was the youngest of five children, and the only one of the family who achieved distinction. His father was a bookseller and publisher, who had had literary aspirations and ambitions beyond his abilities; his mother was a surgeon's daughter, of some intelligence, but narrow and provincial in her education and opinions, and decidedly contemptuous of musicians and artists generally. Not a promising condition of things in this family for the development of a musical genius. There had been no musical talent in the family heretofore, and there was no musical life or interest there now beyond what was connected with the church and the schools. The town offered few advantages. The best piano teacher there was Professor Kuntzsch of the High School, a pedantic, self-made musician, with the defects of method and the narrow provincialism inevitable in a teacher who had never been well trained and who lived so far from the centres of intellectual and artistic activity as to be but little affected by the currents of musical life of his time.

His talent singular in the family.

Robert did not particularly distinguish himself at school, either in childhood or later, but he began to give evidence of musical gifts very early, and his father was wise enough to send him to Professor Kuntzsch for lessons. But he does not seem to have profited much by the instruction, partly because his teacher was incompetent, partly because the two natures were incompatible, and quite as much because the boy was very badly spoiled, had been indulged as the baby and the family pet, and was too irritable, susceptible and obstinate to learn much of anybody except some one who could have obtained complete mastery of him. This wholesome control he never had. He showed the effects

Failure of his lessons with Professor Kuntzsch.

His faults

of his childish faults to some extent all his life and suffered from them, both as artist and as man.

But there were forces in him which could no more help coming to outward manifestation than a live acorn can help growing into an oak, if it have any soil at all for nourishment. What Robert Schumann might have become if he had been thoroughly disciplined and surrounded by favorable influences in his early years we can only conjecture. What he did become we know; and in spite of weaknesses and defects the world has long since agreed to acknowledge him as one of the great leaders and creative minds of his time. It is possible that the very circumstances which we deplore as apparently unfavorable fostered the originality now so much admired; but it is more than probable that this natural force was too strong to have been crushed by any systematic training, however pedantic, and that such surroundings as Chopin or Mendelssohn had would have developed and enriched his nature and genius without warping or misleading him. But however this may be, Schumann never did become either a thoroughly trained pianist or musician in the ordinary sense.

His playing was always more or less faulty in tone and in execution, and he never attained perfect correctness or ease. His Leipzig teacher, Wieck, wanted him to study harmony systematically, when he first took lessons of him at the age of eighteen, but Robert seemed to think a young fellow who could improvise harmonies on the piano had no need of any system and so left harmony alone, until costly experience taught him that he could not do without it. This was one side of the boy's character; but if he had faults for which he had by and by to pay dearly, he had also traits which were to make him both useful and famous. If he was self-willed and obstinate, he was at any rate *alive;* if he would grow only in his own way, still grow he would and did, and a marvelous growth it was.

Power of reproducing impressions in tones.

In early childhood he showed a wonderful power of reproducing in tones impressions made on his sensibility by persons, scenes and events. In spite of his imperfect execution, he would sit down to his pianoforte and invent melodic figures and phrases so characteristic of the traits of his friends that the likenesses would be recognized at once, and comical enough were some of these tone-portraits. Thus, from the very first, this peculiar phase of the romantic tendency manifested itself in the boy. It was innate and could not be suppressed, and this element of romanticism he cultivated as his special and peculiar field. He was a born romanticist through and through, in every fibre of his being, and it was not at all surprising that he took to German romantic literature as his natural intellectual nutriment and stimulus. His father's shop supplied the means of gratifying this taste, and he availed himself of his privileges with the greatest avidity.

His innate romanticism.

But Schumann, if he worked only in his own way, did, nevertheless, work. If he did not plague himself much with Professor Kuntzsch's instructions, he

His self-directed work.

collected round him all the music-loving youths of his acquaintance, played with them in four-hand arrangements a great deal of Haydn, Mozart, Beethoven, Weber, Hummel, Czerny, in short, whatever came to hand in the way of music, composed a great deal in an exceedingly amateurish sort of way, even organized a small orchestra and gave concerts, he conducting and filling in on the pianoforte the parts which were lacking; made attempts at literary authorship, too, wrote robber-plays and produced them on an improvised stage, and altogether showed great and incessant intellectual activity.

His father's plans for him.

All this his father encouraged, and determining to make a musician of him, he wrote to Carl Maria von Weber, asking him to take charge of Robert's musical education. Weber consented, readily enough, but for some reason, the boy never went to him. He floundered along as best he could, pursuing his school studies, his reading and his music in a confused, desultory, hap-hazard way, but with a vast amount of energy and enthusiasm. He was

Harmful effects of his pre-eminence in Zwickau.

acknowledged as the leading spirit, in the field he had chosen, among all the amateurs of Zwickau, and this acknowledged pre-eminence contributed no little to confirm in him the habit of self-will and over-confidence in his own knowledge. It is indeed astonishing, and a signal proof of the greatness of his gifts, that he should ever have come to anything.

The first serious obstacle in the way of his self-chosen path had to be met soon after the death of his father, which occurred when he was sixteen years old. His mother would not hear of his becoming a musician, though she had no objection to his using music as a recreation and amusement. His guardian, a merchant of Zwickau, agreed with her, and the two decided that Robert must go to Leipzig to study law at the university, as soon as he had graduated from the Zwickau grammar school. To Leipzig accordingly he went in March, 1828, and seemed not indisposed to yield to his mother's wishes in the matter of a profession. It is probable that he really meant to attend the lectures on jurisprudence; in fact, he made several attempts to do so, but he never got farther than the door. His time was spent in playing and composing music, attending the Gewandhaus concerts and the opera, making music with a few young student friends and reading, mainly Jean Paul Richter, for whose works he had conceived a violent passion. He further diversified his experience by falling in love with various pretty girls here and there, a species of sentimental indulgence to which he was very prone during all the early part of his life, and which seems to have harmed no one, perhaps not even himself.

He also took a journey to Heidelberg during this spring, in company with Rosen, a young student with whom he had become sworn friends, and passing through Munich met Heinrich Heine and the painter Zimmerman, from both of whom he received impressions which had no little effect upon him. Rosen remained in Heidelberg and the two friends began a correspondence in which the eighteen-year

Marginalia: Chap. IX. Is sent to Leipzig to study law. Journey to Heidelberg.

CHAP. IX.

His morbid sentimentality.

old Schumann appeared mainly as a gushing youth, running over with Jean Paulism and with that peculiar German sentimentality which never fails to strike an Anglo Saxon as somewhat ridiculous and contemptible, but which is perhaps an indispensable element of the German "Gemuethlichkeit," and possibly may even be at the bottom of the pre-eminence of the German race in the development of music as a language of the sensibility.* But these letters also contain premonitions of power, imaginative and intellectual, and show the strong tendency to fantastic dreaming and romantic imagining and feeling which were born in him and were fostered into luxuriant growth by his reading and associations.

His intercourse with Wieck.

One of the most healthful influences which affected him during this year in Leipzig was his intercourse with Friedrich Wieck and his family. Wieck was an extremely original, sensible, active-minded and successful music teacher. He had two daughters, the elder of whom Schumann afterward married. She was at this time about nine years of age and was already an accomplished pianist. Wieck himself was a healthy, merry, wholesome sort of man, the reverse of the tearful, melancholy, over-sentimental temperament of Schumann. The young student spent many delightful hours with the family, profited by his intercourse with them in many ways, and was greatly stimulated by the gifted

---

*See letters in the "Life of Robert Schumann," by von Wasielwski, translated by A. L. Alger, and published by O. Ditson & Co., Boston.

artist nature and precocious attainments of the little Clara.

But this did not last long. Robert left Leipzig for Heidelberg in May, 1829, ostensibly to attend lectures on jurisprudence in the university. What he really did was to practice the piano, partly on the basis of his lessons with Wieck, study and compose music, play a great deal in a select circle of his student friends and a little in public, and devote himself almost exclusively to his musical and literary pursuits. The most significant compositions of this year which now remain to us were numbers 1, 3, 4, 6 and 8 of the "Papillons," a series of short pieces intended to reproduce the impressions of different scenes and incidents at a masked ball.

He does not seem to have yet arrived at any decision as to whether he would ultimately pursue the career of a professional musician; he simply drifted along, yielding to the impulses which moved him in the line of musical activity and almost wholly neglecting his law studies, for which he felt an unconquerable aversion. But matters could not go on so. At the end of the school year something had to be settled, and by this time he had thoroughly made up his mind as to his course. He wrote to his mother, July 30, 1830, informing her of his unwillingness to continue his law studies and his desire to devote himself to music, begged her to write to Wieck for his opinion as to the wisdom of his change of plan, and promised to abide by his old teacher's decision. The letter was modest and respectful, but very decided, and his mother, unwillingly enough, complied with his request. Wieck's reply settled the matter. He assured Mme. Schumann that Robert had abilities which warranted him in expecting to become a great musician, and advised that he be thoroughly educated with this end in view.

He returns to Leipzig to study music with Wieck.

The result of it was that in a few weeks he was again in Leipzig under the guidance of his old instructor, than whom no more competent man could have been selected. He took up his residence in Wieck's house, planning for a thorough course of study of the pianoforte. But this soon came to an end by his ill-advised attempts to shorten the process of technical attainment. Just what were the mechanical appliances he used for this purpose no one seems to know, but, at any rate, his right hand became permanently lame, and he was forced to turn his attention exclusively to composition. His previous efforts in this field, although exhibiting innate power and originality, and displaying the peculiar bent of his mind, had been crude, and he himself had begun to see the necessity of solid theoretical study and practice. By Wieck's advice he put himself under the instruction of Heinrich Dorn, then conductor of the opera and a sound musician, and entered upon the study of harmony and counterpoint with great enthusiasm.

Lames his right hand.

Studies with Dorn.

His lessons with Dorn profited him greatly, but he was nearly twenty-two years old and had lost much precious time. At the same age Mendelssohn was one of the most accomplished musicians in Europe, while Schumann found that the years in which it might have been possible for him to acquire a similar mastery of the technic of composition had passed forever. He never gained any such freedom and facility of expression or command of his musical materials as characterized his future colleague in the Leipzig conservatory.

Schumann soon left Wieck's house, though his intimacy with the family continued, and lived much as other students did. He worked hard days and devoted his evenings to recreation with his friends. Socially he was reserved, or rather impassive, unresponsive, and to all outward appearance apathetic; but his intimates knew that this lethargic exterior covered a sensibility extremely open to impressions of every sort, a keen and subtle perception, a vigorous intellect, a strong sense of humor, a vivid imagination especially delighting in the fantastic and the fanciful, and strong, deep feeling.

His manners and social relations.

These qualities found their fullest revelation and most characteristic embodiment in his music. His "Papillons" ("Butterflies"), op. 2, begun in Heidelberg and finished in Leipzig in 1831, are thoroughly characteristic of his nature and tendencies. They are, in form, a mere series of short pieces, some of them of no great intrinsic significance, but with a poetic intention underlying the separate pieces and the arrangement of them, to which Schumann has given us a clue only by a hint or two, and by a few words of explanation in the last number of the series.

His "Papillons" characteristic.

CHAP. IX.

They suggest the scenes of a masked ball.

But this last is sufficient to show clearly that he intended these pieces to express different phases of feeling induced by the scenes of a masquerade.

The short opening number seems to express the mood appropriate to the first impression made by the lighted ball-room with its throng of pleasure seekers; No. 2 shows us the antics of a harlequin; No. 3, a general promenade or procession of the maskers; No. 7, a tender dialogue between two lovers, followed in No. 8 by the most blissful of waltzes, thoroughly poetic and profoundly suggestive; No. 12 shows us the party breaking up during the final dancing of the "Grandfather" minuet; while the town clock strikes six, the sounds gradually die away one after the other. The remaining numbers are much less suggestive of definite scenes, but those above mentioned can hardly be mistaken.

They show clearly the poetic bent of his mind.

These "Papillons" are interesting and important mainly as showing the bent of his mind toward connecting his music with more or less definitely conceived scenes. This tendency shows itself plainly in many of his works, notably in the Davidsbuendler, op. 6; The Carnival, op. 9; the Fantasy pieces, op. 12; the Scenes from Childhood, op. 15; the Vienna Carnival Pranks, op. 26; the Album for Youth, op. 68; the Forest Scenes, op. 82, and the Album Leaves, op. 124. It is true, he himself has cautioned us, somewhat obscurely, against carrying our literalness of interpretation too far, saying that some of the titles in the Scenes from Childhood were added after the pieces were written, instead of serving beforehand as images which raised the feelings embodied in the music. But his applying the titles showed that he considered them sufficiently appropriate to serve as more or less accurate guides and helps in interpretation, and proves none the less conclusively the poetic tendency of his mind, and his proneness to link scenes and feelings together in his music. That he often did not connect them except in a vague way is thoroughly characteristic.

Schumann was a strong but not a clear thinker, and seldom attained complete mastery of his thought or definite, clear, finished expression, either in music or in literary composition. His was one of those somewhat exasperating yet stimulating minds, of which so many are to be found even among the greatest poets and philosophers of Germany, whose ideas are hopelessly befogged, although they evidently have ideas extremely significant and perhaps all the more attractive that they are incompletely revealed. These minds struggle with their thought, they show unquestionable power, and the very violence of the effort convinces us of the greatness of the ideas; but they are never completely triumphant; they never fully succeed in dragging out into clear daylight and exhibiting in its full proportions what they have discovered; more remains than they themselves have perceived, much less displayed to others; the whole is attractive but tantalizing. This will be best appreciated by those who have tried to make their way through the obscure pages of Hegel in the hope of understanding him. Such are apt to come away convinced that the great philosopher was a long way from understanding his own writing, but also convinced that he had found much worth understanding, and feeling that, on the whole, the attempt had been a bracing, stimulating intellectual effort, not without result in increase of strength and enlargement of ideas

Schumann aims to suggest images by his music.

Schumann undoubtedly aimed often, if not generally, at the utmost definiteness of emotional expression, and often aimed, too, at suggesting definite images by means of expressing in tones the emotional impression made by such images. So that when he inscribes a title which irresistibly suggests a scene or event, we are fairly entitled to follow out the connection with the music as definitely as we can, in the absence of information or direction to the contrary. Enough will remain obscure when we have found every imaginable point of contact.

The "Etudes Symphoniques."

It is perhaps not important here to mention Schumann's minor compositions in detail. Those between the "Papillons" and the "Etudes Symphoniques," op. 13, are of comparatively little importance. These "Etudes, in the form of Variations," were written in 1834, and are not only a great advance on any of his previous works but are among the most profoundly significant and atractive of all his compositions. The gain is not specially in clearness of statement, but in fertility of invention, in wealth of suggestion and in the irresistible impression of depth and power of feeling, intellect and character which they make. In these there is

Their extraordinary power.

no trace of the lachrymose sentimentality so plentiful in his letters; the Schumann of the "Etudes Symphoniques" is hardly to be recognized as the author of the letters to Henrietta Voigt on pages 88-90 of Wasielwski's Life, for example; there is, to be sure, the same fantastic, obscure imagining and moods more or less akin, but the music is vastly stronger and more manly than the letters appear to be. Yet both are productions of the same man at about the same time.

In form, these "Etudes," though called "variations" are very far from conforming to the accepted models, and indeed most of them have so little formal relation to the theme that the term "variation" is almost a misnomer. They are rather Schumann's comments on the original subject (which, by the way, is not his own, but was written by the father of of one of his young lady friends, Baroness Ernestine von Fricken)—pieces suggested to his imagination by the mood of this theme.

This work was immediately followed by the "Carnival," op. 9, another attempt to express in short pieces a series of moods appropriate to a masquerade. The two Sonatas, op. 11 and op. 22, belong to the year 1835. They are much less successful than the pieces just mentioned. Schumann was no master either of the sonata form or of the art of thematic treatment, and his genius was hampered by the classical harness. The op. 22 is much the better of the two.

Between this time and the time of his marriage to

Clara Wieck, in 1840, he wrote the "Kreisleriana," op. 16 (so named from their imaginary connection with Kapellmeister Kreisler, in E. T. A. Hoffmann's fantastic romance, "Kater Murr"), the noble "Fantasia," op. 17; the "Novelettes," op. 21, the "Fantasy Pieces," op. 12; the "Scenes from Childhood," op. 15; "Arabeske," op. 18; "Flower Piece," op. 19; "Humoreske," op. 20; "Night Pieces, op. 23; "Vienna Carnival Pranks," op. 26, and other pieces of minor importance.

This list comprises nearly all his significant works for the pianoforte alone. They were largely the product of a time of mental agitation due to his love affairs. He had wished to marry Ernestine von Fricken and had been very intimate with her when she lived at Wieck's. But for some unexplained reason the connection was broken off, she went home, Schumann fell under Wieck's displeasure and ceased to visit the family. Meanwhile he fell in love with Clara, and after a while she reciprocated his affections, but her father would never consent to receive Schumann as his son-in-law. When the young couple finally did marry, Schumann had to resort to the courts to get possession of his bride.

But Schumann's love affairs and activity in composition by no means occupied all his attention. He was thoroughly disgusted with the shallow criticism and the equally shallow appreciation of music at that time prevalent in Leipzig and elsewhere. The popular pianoforte composers were Kalkbrenner,

Huenten, Herz, Czerny and men of that stamp, whose only merit consisted in a certain amount of pleasing melodiousness without depth of feeling or intelligence. These were, in university student parlance, "Philistines," the natural enemies of originality, genius, and the vigorous individual life which characterized the young Romanticists.

The "Philistines."

Against all pedants, shallow, self-seeking virtuosi and empty-headed, frivolous pianoforte tinklers Schumann determined to wage vigorous war, and entered the field of criticism. In 1834 he, in company with a few like-minded associates, among whom was Wieck, founded the "New Journal of Music" (Neue Zeitschrift fuer Musik), and edited it for ten years. It at once became a great power in musical matters, profoundly influenced public opinion, and introduced to Germany many new writers, among them Chopin, Berlioz, Gade, Stephen Heller, Adolph Henseult, Robert Franz and Sterndale Bennett. Schumann's own writing was much of it fantastic and fanciful; he personified the two sides of his nature under the names of *Florestan* and *Eusebius*, and his associates Wieck and Carl Banck under those of *Raro* and *Serpentinus*, and these imaginary characters are continually appearing in the pages of the journal. The name "Davidsbuendler" or "David and his confederates" also appears, and his "Carnival" contains a "March of the Davidsbuendler against the Philistines." But if he wrote fancifully and more or less obscurely, his criticisms are almost always striking and suggest-

Schumann founds and edits the "Neue Zeitschrift fuer Musik."

ive, and many of them are very clear and forcible. Most of them have been translated into English by Mrs. Fanny Raymond Ritter, and are published in two volumes under the title "Music and Musicians." To these the reader is referred for further knowledge of Schumann's work as a critic.

From the date of his marriage, Schumann's work as a composer concerns this history but little. In that year his emotions found vent in the production of a large number of songs, some of them among the most poetic and imaginative ever written, truthful in characterization, surcharged with profound feeling, and of great beauty. He then began to write for orchestra, and henceforth to the end of his life the piano occupied with him a subordinate place. But among the comparatively few pianoforte compositions of the last sixteen years of his life, there are three very important ones. These are the Pianoforte Quintet, op. 44, the Quartet, op. 47 and the A minor concerto, op. 54, all of them beautiful, significant and original; so much so, indeed, that they can hardly be said to have been surpassed in power by even Beethoven's best work, though they fall far short of the finish of the older master. Besides his songs and orchestral work he also wrote an opera, "Genevieve," which shows great creative power, but has fatal defects as a musical drama, and two cantatas, one "Paradise and the Peri," founded on an episode in Moore's "Lalla Rookh," and the other an adaption of Byron's "Manfred," besides works of minor importance.

In 1843, at Mendelssohn's invitation, he joined him as a teacher of composition, etc., in the newly founded Leipzig conservatory. But this connection did not long continue. Schumann was no teacher; had no power of expressing ideas in speech or of communicating information; was always silent, and apparently apathetic in the class-room as in society. This tendency even increased after his marriage.

In his domestic relations he was happy. Clara Schumann was a woman of genius, the daughter of a man who had known how to develop her gifts in the wisest way; her culture was broad and deep; she was, and still remains (1883), at past sixty, one of the greatest and finest of interpretative artists in an age exceptionally productive of great virtuosi; she was not only exceptionally fitted to be the companion of a great creative mind like Robert Schumann's in all his intellectual and artistic interests and activities, but was a domestic, homelike wife and mother, who stood between her husband and outside annoyances and interruptions, made a delightful, happy, restful home for him and their eight children, and was in every way a woman who commanded and still commands the respect, admiration and love of all who have the felicity of knowing her personally, as well as of thousands who only know her by her admirable performances and her reputation. The present writer looks back upon some concerts of hers with the Gewandhaus orchestra, some sixteen years ago, as among the greatest privileges and most delightful experiences of his life.

Chap. IX.

Schumann's domestic happiness.

With such domestic surroundings it is not to be wondered at that Schumann felt less than ever any inclination for general society. He stayed at home and devoted himself to composition, occasionally going on a concert tour with his wife, who still desired to play in public.

In 1844, Schumann gave up his paper and removed to Dresden. He had already begun to feel the disease which finally destroyed his reason and his life; it was afterwards found to be an abnormal growth of bone into the substance of the brain; it caused him intense pain and occasioned a morbid state of feeling and of mental activity. In 1850 he

His Conductorship at Duesseldorf.

was called to Duesseldorf as director of concerts and church music and accepted the post. But he was never a good conductor, and the progress of his disease made him even less successful than formerly, so that after some three years, a period prolonged somewhat out of consideration for his feelings, the connection terminated.

Insanity and death.

He had almost reached the end. Decided symptoms of insanity developed more and more rapidly and culminated in an attempt at suicide. On February 27, 1854, while sitting in social intercourse with his physician and another friend, he left the room, without a word, went to the bridge and threw himself into the Rhine. He was rescued, but his mind was gone. He was removed to a private asylum near Bonn, and died there July 29, 1856.

A brief comparison of the three great composers whose creative activity determined the course of

Musical History in the Romantic Epoch must close this chapter. All three were subjective; each consciously and deliberately sought to reproduce his emotional life in tones; each embodied in his compositions his most peculiar experiences; so that in the music of each is revealed his innermost life and character.

Chap. IX.
The Romantic writers compared.

Of the three, Mendelssohn was the most healthy and wholesome; dealt less with social emotions of the feverish, abnormally exciting sort; was closer to nature, too, and to the healthiest literature. His Midsummer Night's Dream music is perhaps his most characteristic work, where he deals with nature in her romantic aspects; his imagination is kindled by the solemn grandeur of the forest, the mysterious gloom and silence of night, broken only by the cry of night birds and of insects, the dewy, moonlit glades, the flowery nooks, the thick coverts, the fairy train of Oberon and Titania, with mischievous Puck and the other attendants, the lovers whose transitory mishaps only enhance the charm of the scene, the clumsy clowns rehearsing their play, Bottom, with the ass's head and the fairy queen's ridiculous infatuation with him.

Mendelssohn.

Love of Nature shown in Midsummer Night's Dream.

But hardly less characteristic are his lovely, romantic four-part songs, his overtures and symphonies. The love of natural scenery reappears in these works and in the Walpurgis Night, and his oratorios show a noble, elevated religious life, such as nowhere appears in Schumann or Chopin. The majestic figure of the Prophet and the fiery enthusi-

A religious life shown in his Oratorios.

asm of the Apostle inspired him as no similar characters affected his two romantic contemporaries. The social emotions, too, expressed in his songs, with and without words, are natural and under rational control, never become overmastering passions, are always the revelation of a happy, sunny, joyous, yet serious and thoughtful nature.

Chopin, on the other hand, has little apparent relation either to nature or to religion. His emotional life is conditioned solely on social relations, and those not always of the healthiest or most elevated. He is sometimes morbidly intense, delirious, passionate; there is pleasure intoxicating to the verge of delirium; his pain, grief and despair occasionally border on insanity; in short, the passions of Polish and Parisian society, the whole emotional life of a passionate, worldly, intellectual, refined, luxurious, pleasure-seeking aristocracy is mirrored in his music. It impresses us, too, with a sense of what it would be somewhat unjust to call weakness or effeminacy; it is rather a deficiency of robustness and virility, a character tender, refined, almost feminine, but yet with a vast reserve fund of power and with a certain positiveness and vigor which goes far to make up for his over-sensitiveness and susceptibility to outside influences.

Above all, Chopin is always an artist; his sense of beauty is keen and subtle; his feeling for form is an unerring instinct; his power of invention, both in melody and harmony, is unsurpassed; and the exquisite beauty of many, indeed most, of his works will for long remain a source of delight to connoisseurs.

Schumann's greatest deficiencies, as already pointed out, are lack of clearness, definiteness, concentration, and imperfect mastery of his means of expression. What he had to express, however, was an emotional life more virile, robust, powerful than that of either Chopin or Mendelssohn. The fire of Chopin's passion glowed with equal intensity, but the impulse it gave was more fitful and spasmodic. Schumann's feeling rushes on with all-compelling, resistless force; even when imperfectly revealed it is Titanic; if we sometimes get no more than glimpses of his passion, even these convince us that there is not only intensity but mass of heat, like a vast furnace full of molten metal, from which indeed run great masses of slag and dross, but these are the very result and product of huge purification. With all his passion, his intense longing, strong out-reaching desire, earnest striving, headlong impulse, there is a sense of repose which comes only from the working of a great force.

The passion of Chopin is violent, rushing, impetuous, but carries less weight. Or, to change the figure—Schumann's passion rolls in great, deep-sea waves, which break on rocky cliffs in thunderous roar of overwhelming surf; Chopin's is a narrow tropical sea, beautiful in calm and sunshine, but fruitful of sudden hurricanes and violent storms, of deafening thunder and blinding electric flashes; Mendelssohn's is an inland lake, not too deep to be

Schumann

His profound and vigorous feelings.

Comparison of the passion of the three writers.

easily fathomed, with charming, quiet bays and enticing nooks haunted by sprites and elves, a veritable fairy domain, the abode of grace and beauty. All three are to be counted among the world's great and precious treasures. "Romantic" they are, certainly; but if it can ever be possible to judge of the permanence of any contemporary Art, then may we surely expect that these three great masters will by and by be counted as "classics." At any rate their place in musical history is unmistakable.

PART FOURTH.

The Development of Pianoforte Technic.

CHAPTER X.

THE TECHNIC OF THE FIRST CLASSICAL PERIOD.

When the harpsichord was invented we know not. But we do know that the organ preceded it. The harpsichord seems to have been, at first, a mere household substitute for the organ, which latter instrument was, of course, too large and expensive to be used anywhere except in churches, monasteries and other large places for public assemblies. The harpsichord was at first a resource of organists for home practice and gradually found its way into popular use.

Relation of the harpsi- chord to the organ.

At first, organ music was transferred to it, and no account was taken of its peculiar capabilities. For a long time pieces were written "for the organ or harpsichord," and even at the time of Bach and Haendel harpsichord players were almost always organists as well. And not only so, but these players seem to have considered the organ as so much superior that they devoted little attention to the harpsichord, regarding it as a mere auxiliary, subordinate to their main interests.

But the striking difference between the capacities of the two instruments must have suggested to some of these players that there might be something in the harpsichord worth cultivating. So long as scien-

Beginnings of harpsi- chord music proper.

CHAP. X.

Shortness of tone necessitated ornaments.

Effect of lack of sonority.

tific music was almost exclusively confined to the service of the church, so long the organ retained its exclusive supremacy. But when opera was invented, in the sixteenth century, and the harpsichord not only came into prominent use in the orchestra, but had to serve for the accompaniments of recitatives and arias, its importance increased. Compositions began to be written which took into account its special peculiarities; its evanescent tones, its lack of sonority and its lightness and shallowness of touch as compared with the clumsy actions of the organs of the period.

The shortness of the tones precluded the cultivation of the lyric quality and suggested the appropriateness of rapid passages as the staple element of compositions intended for that instrument. When tones had to be prolonged they were trilled or furnished with turns, mordents, prall-trills or appoggiaturas. These were borrowed from the vocal embellishments of the time, but were not mere ornaments, as in the case of arias, etc.; they served to supply the defect of shortness of tone in the instrument, and so were an important element in harpsichord music.

The second peculiarity, lack of sonority, owing to the lightness of the strings and the impossibility of producing a powerful tone by plucking a string with a quill, precluded any broad, majestic effects, and contributed to the adoption of light and rapid passages and embellishments as the main peculiarities of harpsichord music.

TECHNIC OF THE FIRST CLASSICAL PERIOD. 183

Lastly, the lightness of the action pointed in the same direction.

Harpsichord technic, then, involved light and rapid playing of scales and arpeggios and of all sorts of finger passages, including trills and other embellishments. It required independence and flexibility of the fingers and great dexterity, but not strength.

But there was no employment of extended scales and arpeggios as there is in our modern music. In the first place, these instruments were much smaller in compass than our modern pianofortes, rarely exceeding five octaves.

Then, too, the prevalent music was polyphonic, and extended passages were impossible in fugue playing. Each hand had generally to perform two or more voice-parts at the same time, and this involved the necessity of writing them within a narrow range of notes.

It was perhaps owing to this fact that the fingering of single scale passages in vogue at that time was so crude and clumsy. As late as the last decade of the seventeenth century the rules laid down in the instruction books for fingering scales required them to be played with *two* fingers only; the third (middle) and fourth in ascending and the third and second in descending.

The use of all five fingers was a result of the development of monophonic playing, or, what is, for technical purposes, the same thing, of the employment of long passages for only one voice for a single

CHAP. X.

What was involved in harpsichord technic.

Limitations.

Crude fingering.

How improvements were made.

hand, in free polyphony. The hand, not being hampered by the necessity of playing two or more voices, could indulge in much greater freedom of execution, and out of this gradually came florid monophony, culminating at last in our day in the difficult passages of Thalberg, Liszt and others.

Bach's free polyphony.

Of this style of free polyphony involving florid monophonic passages Sebastian Bach was as great a master as he was of strict polyphonic playing. In the latter he was unrivaled. He was not only the greatest composer of fugues, but the greatest player of fugues. In the art of delivering several melodies simultaneously he surpassed all his predecessors and contemporaries. This art involved the frequent changing of fingers on one key and the sliding of the fingers from one key to another, so as to produce a perfect connection between the tones.

Artistic capabilities of the clavichord.

The greatest defect of the harpsichord for fugue playing was the impossibility of discriminative emphasis. The clavichord was somewhat superior in this respect. It was possible to make some slight difference in the power of the tones of this instrument, to emphasize somewhat the entrance of a fugue subject or answer, and to discriminate one melody or passage from another by greater or less force of delivery. Above all, it was superior to the harpsichord in *lyric* quality, in the possibility of prolonging the tones beyond a mere tinkle, and imparting to them something of singing effect.

Accordingly, the clavichord was a favorite instrument with Sebastian Bach, as having finer artistic capabilities than either the harpsichord or the pianofortes of his day. The action of the latter was still too imperfect and clumsy to satisfy his requirements. The mechanism of the pianoforte is necessarily complicated, and it was thirty or forty years after Bach's death before it finally superseded the older instruments.

Sebastian Bach's technic, then, was the technic of the harpsichord, and especially of the clavichord. In him polyphonic playing, as well as polyphonic writing, culminated. All that could be done on the instruments of his time he did. He attained the utmost independence of finger, the utmost ease, lightness, fluency; his dexterity in interweaving contrapuntal parts was perfection itself; he employed all five fingers in passages when they could be used to advantage, disregarding the pedantic rules of his time; he made the most of the lyric capabilities of the clavichord. In short, like most original minds, he was an innovator, discovering all the possibilities of the instruments he used and inventing new means of accomplishing his ends.

Bach's technic.

Haendel was also a great organist and harpsichordist, but devoted most of his life to the production of Italian opera. His harpsichord technic, as far as it goes, differs in no essential particular from Bach's.

Haendel's technic.

Domenico Scarlatti seems to have had more of the virtuoso spirit, in the sense in which that term is used in Germany at the present day.

Scarlatti's virtuosity.

A virtuoso, in this sense, is one who puts the

mastery of technical difficulties and the display of his technical attainments above those aims which the real artist regards as paramount.

The true artist has in view, first of all, the worthy embodiment of a worthy ideal. As an interpretative artist he holds it his paramount duty to render truthfully the conceptions of any composer whose works he takes upon himself to represent to others, selecting the works of no composer whose genius he does not respect, treating them reverently and interpreting them with conscientious fidelity, so far as he can ascertain the composer's intention.

The virtuoso, on the other hand, is apt to use his attainments primarily as a means of glorifying himself in the eyes of others. Whatever he writes is apt to be written with reference to the display of his attainments, to the production of astonishing and sensational effects, that he may gain glory for himself. His performances of the compositions of others are apt to be characterized by the same dominant purpose. "*Effect*" is the watchword of the virtuoso. He does not like to play pieces, however noble or significant, which are not "*effective.*" He is apt to desecrate the noblest works of the greatest genius by additions and alterations intended solely for show.

The spirit of the artist is one of self-abnegation, of devotion to ideal aims. The virtuoso is primarily an egotist, using his technical attainments as a means not to the faithful setting forth of noble conceptions, but for his own personal aggrandizement.

But, although there are abundant examples of both classes of players, there are perhaps few artists who play much in public without sometimes being tempted to sacrifice something of the higher interests they are called to represent, to the desire for applause, and perhaps there are few virtuosi who do not sometimes feel impelled to use their splendid gifts and acquirements for high ends. It is a question, in each individual case, of predominant tendency and habitual intention.

As regards Domenico Scarlatti, it would doubtless be very unjust to represent him as a virtuoso pure and simple, in the sense in which that word has just been explained. But there is much in his compositions which seems to have been conditioned, not on any inward necessity of expression, but on the desire to overcome technical difficulties and to display his mastery of them. There are passages exceedingly troublesome to players even now, which seem to serve no ideal end, but to exist solely for the sake of difficulty.

Evidences of the virtuoso spirit.

The most conspicuous examples of this are passages where the hands are crossed very rapidly, as in the sonata No. 10 of Koehler's edition (see Chapter I). But whatever we may think of the intellectual or artistic worth of this sort of work, it undoubtedly contributed much to the mastery of technic, and especially to the development of the monophonic style of playing.

CHAPTER XI.

THE TECHNIC OF THE SECOND CLASSICAL PERIOD.

Chap. XI. The change in technic gradual.

When we compare the sonatas of Scarlatti, the suites of Haendel and the suites, partitas, sonatas and concertos of Sebastian Bach with the sonatas of Emanuel Bach, we find no sudden change in technical qualities. Indeed, the development of the technic of the pianoforte was a slow and gradual process, and neither Emanuel Bach, Haydn nor Mozart ever fully recognized the peculiar capacities of the new instrument. All three were bred harpsichordists, and even in the Mozart concertos, the culmination of technic in these three authors, most of the passages are perfectly practicable for the harpsichord. In these works, as in those of Haydn and Emanuel Bach, we find the same demand for lightness and fluency which characterized the concertos and other compositions of Sebastian Bach's time.

Characteristics of the Vienna pianoforte.

This was, in part, due to the fact that the Vienna pianofortes had very light actions, modeled on those of the harpsichords then in use. The ideals of pianoforte technic and effects were drawn from the experience of harpsichord players, modified only by the single consideration of the possibility of shading. But this capacity for varying the power of tones was an element which gradually enlarged the ideas of players as to the possible effects derivable from it, and, after a while, led to great changes in the construction of the instrument.

Nevertheless, Vienna was not the place where these modifications first suggested themselves; the Viennese players and composers continued for a long time to be the exponents of a smooth, easy-going, superficial style of technic and of playing, and the Viennese pianofortes continued to be very light in action and lacking in sonority, making small demands on the power and endurance of players, and incapable of broad or powerful effects.

From the above judgment of Viennese composers, Beethoven, and in a less degree, Schubert must be excepted. More of these hereafter.

The most important service rendered by Emanuel Bach, Haydn and Mozart in the development of pianoforte technic was their progressive recognition of the *lyric* element. The *adagios* in the sonatas of Emanuel Bach were distinct attempts to improve upon the singing effects already attained on the clavichord. They were probably calculated for that instrument, at least quite as much as for the pianoforte, for, although Bach played both instruments, and the harpsichord as well, he is said always to have preferred certain effects obtainable on the clavichord to any of those which could be produced by the pianofortes of his day.

The most peculiar of these effects was the "*Bebung*," a peculiar tremulous effect produced by a rapid repetition of slight pressure on the key. The "Tangent," which was in contact with the string as long as the key was held down, transmitted this vibratory motion to the string, producing an effect probably analogous to that with which we are familiar in the playing of violinists and violoncellists.

But although Bach preferred the clavichord for the performance of his lyric pieces, the stress he laid upon the lyric element in playing must have tended strongly to develop the lyric capabilities of the pianoforte, an instrument which was now rapidly growing in favor, so much so as to fairly supersede the older instruments about the time of Emanuel Bach's death (1788).

How Haydn and Mozart developed technic.

Haydn and Mozart also cultivated the lyric element of the pianoforte. Their works show a steady development of it. Haydn modeled on Bach, and Mozart on Bach and Haydn, and in the Mozart sonatas and concertos we find what was probably a full and complete recognition of the lyric possibilities of the small, light Viennese pianofortes of his time.

The extended scale and arpeggio passages of the Mozart concertos also show a distinct recognition of the capabilities of light and shade peculiar to the pianoforte, although their relation to the harpsichord is almost as close as their relation to the newer instruments.

But there was an Italian contemporary of his who, though he was no such original genius as Mozart, rendered more important service than he in the development of pianoforte technic. This was MUZIO CLEMENTI (1752–1832), an artist and virtuoso who occupies somewhat the same relation to Mozart and Haydn that Domenico Scarlatti did to Bach and Haendel.

Clementi, 1752-1832.

He was born at Rome, went to England in his childhood and spent most of his lifetime there. His eighty years were full of honorable and useful activity. He was a thorough musician, an excellent composer, so far as technical attainments went, and had very marked talent, so much, indeed, that no less a judge than Beethoven preferred his sonatas to Mozart's. He composed about a hundred sonatas, the same number of studies (Gradus ad Parnassum), besides symphonies, choruses, etc.

He was a superior teacher, and formed some of the finest pianists of the next generation; among them J. B. Cramer, John Field, Alex. Klengel and Ludwig Berger. He also conducted Italian opera in London, and engaged in the manufacture of pianofortes.

In early life, he aimed at brilliant execution, and especially cultivated difficult playing in double thirds, fourths, sixths and octaves. He afterwards acquired a broad *cantabile* and a nobler and more artistic style generally. He was a pianist rather than a harpsichordist, and was really the first of the great players of whom this could be said. He preferred the English pianofortes with their heavy action, and adapted his playing and his compositions to these instruments.

As player.

CHAP. XI.

Clementi's technic as related to English pianofortes.

These English pianos had greater sonority than those of Vienna; the heavier stroke suggested heavier strings and a larger sounding-board, and they required a technic approaching that of the modern instruments. It is Clementi's great contribution to pianoforte technics that he fully apprehended the requirements and capacities of the best English instruments of his day, and in his playing, teaching, and composing, gave them adequate recognition.

His importance in the history of technic.

The whole fabric of modern pianoforte technic rests on the *Gradus ad Parnassum*. Up to the compositions of Chopin, Liszt and Schumann, there is nothing for which these studies do not afford an adequate foundation. Even the Beethoven Fifth Concerto does not go beyond the Clementi technic, in its principles or its extreme difficulty.

Clementi's lifetime covers a period from seven years before the death of Haendel to four years after that of Beethoven and up to within two years of the establishment of the *Neue Zeitschrift fuer Musik* by Schumann. He lived through the whole epoch of the development of the sonata, its culmination and transformation, and into the very sunrise of the Romantic epoch.

CHAPTER XII.

THE TECHNIC OF THE TRANSITION PERIOD.

We have already seen that Clementi, the most important factor in the classical technic, lived not only through the first classical period, but through the transition period as well. He was born four years earlier than Mozart and died four years later than Beethoven. Moreover, the most important part of his work was done between the dates of Mozart's death and that of Beethoven.

Although the romantic ideals were pressing into the foreground, the whole technic of the transition period was classical. We have already noticed that Beethoven's most difficult concerto is amply provided for in Clementi's technic.

Beethoven did, indeed, embody a content in the greatest of his works, for the interpretation of which the full resources of our modern instruments are no more than sufficient. In this respect his work is prophetic. But the essential elements of his technic are all to be found in the Gradus of Clementi. One of the most noticeable points of his early technic is his use of rapid successions of chords, as in the Sonata in C, op. 2, No. 3. This is evidently borrowed from Clementi, who was, at that time, his favorite model.

CHAP. XII.

Technic of Schubert and Weber.

The technic of Schubert and Weber was also based on that of Clementi. The latter, however, made use of extended chords in a way wholly original, an example which has been followed since. He also used the octave *glissando* in his " Concert-Stueck," a mere virtuoso trick, which has remained wholly without influence on practice since.

In general, it may be said that not only the contemporaries of Clementi, but all classical players and composers since, have based their technic on his *Gradus ad Parnassum*. Some of them, like Moscheles, for example, have seized upon points which he had treated but briefly and have elaborated them at great length and in detail. Many individual peculiarities of treatment and style are also to be found, and the classical players of the Romantic period could hardly remain wholly unaffected by the innovations of the Romantic composers. But, in principle, all classical technic is to be found in Clementi; and all in our modern playing which cannot be accounted for on his principles can be referred to Liszt and the other Romanticists.

All technic either classical or romantic in principle.

Use of the damper pedal.

In one single point of technic have players, not distinctively Romantic, gone beyond Clementi's practice or suggestion, viz., the use of the damper pedal. Beethoven used it considerably, and Moscheles (1784-1870) still more extensively. Henselt (born 1814) still further enlarged the domain of the pedal, and Thalberg (1812-1871), who cannot be classed as either a classicist or romanticist, but is the culmination of the "Philistine" school of shallow players, of which Czerny and Kalkbrenner were distinguished representatives, carried the use of it to its extreme limits.

CHAPTER XIII.

THE TECHNIC OF THE ROMANTIC PERIOD.

CHAP. XIII.
Persistence of classical technic in the romantic period.

We have already seen that the classical school of playing persisted after the advent of the great Romanticists. Kalkbrenner (1788–1849), one of the greatest of the classical virtuosi, died in the same year with Chopin. Moscheles (1794–1870) outlived all the Romanticists. Hiller was born in 1811, Thalberg in 1812 and Henselt in 1814. Of these three only Thalberg is dead, and even he outlived all the great Romanticists except Liszt. Besides these there is a host of players who are classicists by tradition and principle.

These followers of the methods of classical technic were, indeed, more or less affected by the Romantic influences which surrounded them, but these influences showed themselves rather in attempts at characterization and the embodiment of a Romantic content than in any borrowing of the peculiar effects of the distinctively Romantic technic. Indeed, Mendelssohn himself was essentially a classicist in much of his technic, no less than in the clearness of his forms. Even in the Songs without Words, there is little which cannot be referred back to the technical principles of Clementi.

These principles depended mainly on the con-

THE TECHNIC OF THE ROMANTIC PERIOD. 197

struction of compositions from five-finger passages, scales and arpeggios. The rules of fingering required that a five-key position should always be taken when possible; that a position once taken should not be changed unnecessarily; that all passages derived from scales and arpeggios should be fingered like the arpeggios or scales on which they were founded; that the thumb and little finger, being shorter than the others, should not be used on black keys, except in positions where their shortness produced no disadvantage. These principles suffice for playing all classical compositions in the monophonic style.

Chap. XIII.
Rules of fingering.

But Mendelssohn, in many of his Songs without Words, introduced passages where a melody with an accompaniment to be played by the same hand could be delivered properly only by changing the fingers on successive keys while holding them down with a continuous clinging pressure.

Mendelssohn's technic.

This changing of fingers was not wholly new, for Bach had used it in polyphonic playing, and occasional instances of it had occurred since, in Clementi's works and elsewhere; but with Mendelssohn it assumed new and greater importance. His Songs without Words became the fashion, served as models to many composers, and intensified the already great and growing interest in the purely lyric style.

The clinging touch.

This interest was greatly heightened by the lyric pieces of Chopin. But Chopin's relation to technic was much more important than Mendelssohn's. He was an innovator; as original in his technical meth-

Chopin's technic.
Its originality.

ods and treatment as he was in his ideas and his harmonies. Above all others he thoroughly understood how to write for the pianoforte, and how to produce effects hitherto unattained. He improved the legato playing of chromatic passages, especially in double thirds and other intervals, by putting the fifth finger under the fourth and third in descending and the third and fourth over the fifth in ascending. He showed how to produce a smooth, even chain of tones in arpeggios dispersed in wide intervals, and in extended chords. He wrote arpeggios so interspersed with passing-notes and appoggiaturas that no rules of fingering previously known would apply to them, and showed how they could be played with ease and certainty.

Schumann's technic.

Schumann also had a peculiar technic, but one which seemed, at least, less perfectly adapted to the requirements and resources of the pianoforte. Apparently, his innovations were not, like Chopin's, based on a thorough mastering of all previous technical achievements and a clear perception of new effects to be produced by a further natural development. They were dependent rather on the requirements of emotional expression, to which the pianoforte must adapt itself if it could ; if not, so much the worse for the pianoforte.

Its difficulties.

The new difficulties consisted partly in obscure and involved rhythms, partly in the peculiar relations of the melodies to their accompaniments, partly in the use of extended chords in awkward positions, and partly in the participation of both hands in the delivery of the same phrase.

In all these cases the thought is first in importance with the composer and facility of execution seems to be an entirely subordinate matter.

Schumann's innovations, therefore, had, for a long time, comparatively little influence on the technical treatment of the pianoforte. But of late years, a generation of players and composers has sprung up who have been powerfully affected by the Schumann cultus, and have thoroughly accustomed themselves to his technic. It now begins to be said that some of his powerful effects imply and demand many of the most important technical qualities, both in player and instrument, which have heretofore been credited to Liszt, and which Liszt was certainly the first to popularize, both among players and pianoforte makers. The new school of writers represented by Brahms, Tschaikowsky, Moszkowski, the two Scharwenkas, the Brassin brothers and Sgambati, is deeply marked by the Schumann peculiarities.

Chopin excepted, no composer has wrought such remarkable changes in technic during his life time as FRANZ LISZT. He was born October 22, 1811, at Raiding, near Pesth, in Hungary. His father gave him his first lessons in playing the pianoforte at the age of six years.

The boy at once showed the most remarkable gifts. His sight-reading, comprehension and execution were astonishing. At nine years of age he was able to play a difficult concerto in public, and roused the admiration of all who heard him by the fire and spirit of his performances.

He attracted the attention of two Hungarian noblemen, who gave him a pension of six hundred gulden (about three hundred dollars) a year to enable him to prosecute his studies. His father then took him to Vienna and placed him under Czerny's instruction. The boy also studied theory with old Salieri

His sight reading.

How well he read at sight will appear from a single anecdote. He went one day into a music store where some musicians were examining a new and difficult concerto of Hummel. Knowing that he played almost everything at sight, they gave him this as an extraordinary test. He played it at once with apparent ease.

Of course, for such a pupil there could be few difficulties, and before long young Liszt had completely risen above all the demands of technic as then practised and had begun to invent new effects of his own. He also mastered the whole range of existing compositions for his instrument.

In 1823 his father took him to Paris and the following year to London, in both of which cities his playing excited surprise and admiration.

He settles in Paris.

In 1827 his father died, and young Liszt, now sixteen years of age, went to Paris to seek his fortune as pianist and teacher. He became at once a prominent adherent of the extreme Romantic school.

Soon after he went to Paris, Hector Berlioz pub-

THE TECHNIC OF THE ROMANTIC PERIOD. 201

licly produced some of his fantastic "programme music." Young Liszt was strongly attracted by its peculiar style and impressed by its unquestionable power, as well as by the evident mastery of all the resources of the orchestra displayed by this extremely eccentric and original composer. He soon set to work to transcribe these works for the pianoforte.

The problem he set for himself was to reproduce, with the limited resources of an instrument poor in melody and monotonous in tone-color, the effects of the full orchestra with all its different families of instruments. A stupendous task, indeed, and one impossible to discharge except in remote approximation. But the degree of his success was astonishing, and his playing of his transcriptions was an exhibition of virtuosity which completely threw into the shade the performances of all other virtuosi in the capital. He followed up these works by numerous transcriptions of orchestral works, including some of the Beethoven symphonies, and afterwards transcribed numerous opera melodies, songs by Schubert and others, Hungarian Gypsy melodies (Rhapsodies), and some of Bach's organ fugues.

The impulse to this work was greatly quickened by the violin playing of Paganini, who appeared in Paris in 1831. It was young Liszt's ambition to become the Paganini of the pianoforte. With this end in view he studied and experimented constantly to produce new effects in melody, harmony and brilliant passages, to increase the power and sonority of his touch, to vary the quality or "color" of his

CHAP. XIII.

His transcriptions.

Liszt's Technic.

tones by different kinds of touches, to discriminate the different elements of a piece as widely as possible, and to make his playing effective by violence of contrast, force, fire, spirit, delicacy and refinement, all carried to the highest attainable pitch of excellence. In all this he was successful, and attained such mastery as was not only the despair of all the players of that time, but remains, by general consent, unrivaled by any of the great pianists who have since been formed on the principles of his own technic.

These principles were, first, the development of the greatest possible strength and power of discriminative emphasis in the individual fingers, and second, a much greater use of the hand playing with a loose wrist than had hitherto been customary.

The means he used.

For the first, he held the wrist higher than other players, and left it perfectly flexible, but still in such a position that the fingers had all possible mechanical advantage for the production of a powerful tone. He also invented simple and radical exercises for developing the strength of the fingers in the shortest possible time. For the second, he made great use of single and double trills, runs, arpeggios, interlocking passages, etc., to be executed with the two hands alternately. This produced a totally new class of effects by means of wrist action.

These brilliant pyrotechnics, though really not much more difficult of attainment than the effects of the older technic, were thought at the time to be impossible for any one except Liszt himself, and pieces like his "Rigoletto" Fantasie, now effectively played by some boarding-school misses, were then thought too difficult for great virtuosi.

Between the years 1836 and 1848 Liszt played a great deal in all the principal cities of Europe and even in Constantinople, and was honored as few artists have ever been, alike by kings, princes, nobility and commoners.

In 1848 he became conductor of the Grand Duke's Opera at Weimar and since that has seldom played in public. He gave up his conductorship in 1859, and has since lived at Weimar, Pesth and Rome, always surrounded by friends and admirers, and by young pianists seeking his counsel.

To these he has always shown himself a friend and benefactor.

But Liszt's generosity has never been confined to artists. Wherever there was distress or need, there he was always ready with money, sympathy and powerful influence for help. No artist was ever more loved than he, and none ever seemed more influential in his own time.

Liszt has devoted himself of late years to the composition of great choral and orchestral works. He had previously written many etudes, two concertos and many other original works for the pianoforte. In these pieces, as in his transcriptions, the prime consideration is their relation to the public. His original ideas are seldom or never profoundly significant. Few of his original pianoforte works, at least, are conditioned on an inward necessity for emotional expression so much as on the desire to affect others. And again, the desire is not to affect others by the communication of great thoughts and feelings which press for utterance and crave sympathy, but to make *effect*, to produce sensation, to dazzle, astonish, overwhelm by a display of force, brilliancy and mastery of effects unattainable by others.

His works sensational.

Liszt's works are always exciting, but few of them are poetic or inspiring. They are imposing in their sonority and in the bold and striking character of their effects, and imposing also in the sense that they appear at first to be much more significant than they really are. After we have a little recovered from the first shock of the powerful sensations they produce, we discover that these stormy passages are grandiose, not grand; noisy, not sublime; sensational, not profound.

Effect of his works.

The effect of them and of Liszt's playing and teaching has been to revolutionize technic and to bring about great changes in the construction of the pianoforte in the direction of an enormous increase of sonority and of capacity to endure a powerful touch without injury to the quality of the tone.

But as regards creative and perhaps even interpretative Art, Liszt's influence has been much less marked and does not seem likely to be permanent. After all, the kingdom of true Art, like "the kingdom of God, cometh not with observation," and is manifested not in the fire nor in the whirlwind, but in the "still small voice."

Liszt will certainly be known in the history of pianoforte music as the greatest virtuoso of his time. It seems not improbable that he will be credited with the development of the pianoforte and of its technical requirements to the extreme limits of the possibilities of both. At any rate, it is hard to see any capacities in the present instruments which Liszt has not exhausted, or what possible use of the muscles of the hand and arm in playing he has not discovered and practiced. He is the king of pianists and this title he seems likely to retain for all time.

Liszt's place in history.

To sum up this discussion: Besides the increased demands on the interpretative powers of the player made by the great Romanticists, there are peculiar intellectual requirements. Among these are the peculiar involved, intricate rhythms of Schumann and the extremely original harmonies and modulations of Chopin and Liszt.

Summary.

But when these peculiarities have been perfectly grasped and assimilated in the mind of the player they are seen to involve mechanical difficulties of a character foreign to the classical technic.

Increased demands of modern technic.

1. The great increase of sonority demands greater development of strength in the hand and fingers without in the least impairing the flexibility of the hand and wrist. Indeed the demand for perfect flexibility and independence of all the muscles, joints and nerves involved is even greater

Strength.

than ever, for the demand for discriminative emphasis is greatly increased. Not only must the two hands be perfectly independent of each other, but each separate finger must be able to produce the most powerful tone of which it is capable, while other fingers in the same hand are producing tones of differing degrees of force. In short, there was never before such a demand for the blending of different degrees of force in touch, discriminating each with the greatest precision and nicety.

2. The peculiar harmonies and especially the employment of harmonic bye-tones in scale and arpeggio passages demands a different mode of fingering from that which sufficed for the playing of classical pieces. This fingering involves putting the fourth and fifth fingers under the others with entire freedom, and, in general, a much freer use of the thumb and little finger, especially on the black keys, than was formerly admitted.

3. The greater sonority attained by the use of chords in extended positions demands new stretches of the fingers laterally to make the new intervals effective. This involves both a greater development of the interosseous muscles of the hand, and a new lateral action of the hand from the wrist, some one of the middle fingers being used as an axis on which the hand turns loosely and rapidly to reach its new position. There has also been a great increase in the demand for long skips.

4. The demands for wrist action are also much greater than formerly, both as regards the alternate

employment of the hands in trills and interlocking passages, and as regards full chords struck *staccato*, or in rapid succession.

Two important works intended to develop the necessary technic to meet the demands of the Romantic compositions are worthy of notice here: The Tausig " Daily Studies " and Mason's " Pianoforte Technics."

CARL TAUSIG (1841-1871), was perhaps the most brilliant of all Liszt's pupils. A virtuoso of the very highest rank, for whom absolutely no technical difficulties existed, with a technic which seemed infallible, his performances were dazzling in the extreme. Moreover he was a thoughtful, intelligent, well-educated man and a practical teacher, so that he was every way admirably fitted to embody and communicate the results of his study and experience.

He taught some years in Berlin, and gradually elaborated a system of elementary technical exercises calculated to develop strength, flexibility and in short all the requirements of the modern technic.

He did not live to complete it however. It was finally edited and published by his friend, H. Ehrlich, another prominent teacher and pianist in Berlin, who incorporated many excellent ideas of his own in the work.

These exercises, though seemingly elementary, must be used with great discretion, if at all, in the earlier stages of instruction. They are mainly useful to advanced players under the guidance of an intelligent teacher.

CHAP. XIII.
Mason's Pianoforte Technics.

The Mason Technics, on the other hand, are simple and radical, and can be used with beginners. Indeed, there is no single exercise which will so rapidly develop strength, flexibility of wrist and hand, delicacy, force and discrimination of touch, in short, all the technical merits of good playing, as the two-finger exercise elaborated by Mason in this work. He obtained the first hint of it from Liszt and afterwards developed and amplified it greatly.

The treatment of rhythm in this work is also admirable and exhaustive. The book is one which no teacher can afford to overlook.

Much of the clearness and force of statement which characterize the book, as well as some of the original work, are to be credited to the associate editor, W. S. B. Mathews (author of "How to Understand Music"), who is wholly responsible for the letter press.

Wm. Mason.

DR. WM. MASON, author of the book, was born in 1829, and was a son of the well-known Dr. Lowell Mason. He went to Europe young, studied with Moscheles, Hauptmann and Dreyschock, and then went to Liszt about 1850, remaining with him some time. He became a very distinguished pianist with a world wide reputation. He has been settled as a teacher in New York since 1856, and has written many graceful, refined, excellent pieces for his instrument.

PART FIFTH.
MINOR COMPOSERS AND VIRTUOSI OF THE DIFFERENT EPOCHS.

CHAPTER XIV.

A. THE EPOCH OF POLYPHONIC MUSIC.

The first harpsichord players were organists, and it was a very long time before there was any differentiation of harpsichord music from organ music. Whatever was written for one was played indifferently on the othei

The prevalent style was that of strict polyphony, though the dance forms gradually assumed a more lyric character and approached the monophonic style, developing the simple period forms. The harpsichord was the popular household instrument in Italy, Germany, England, and, indeed, wherever music was cultivated.

Harpsichord music in Italy.

In Italy, Venice was the city where instrumental music was more especially cultivated, and the successive organists of St. Mark's church distinguished themselves also as harpsichord players.

The most celebrated of these was Adrian Willaert, a Netherlander, who founded the Venetian Music School in the first half of the sixteenth century. He wrote "Fantasies" and "Ricercari" in a free contrapuntal style, and was a great musician and composer. In his day, the so-called "Ecclesiastical Keys"* prevailed, and he was among the first to

Willaert.

*See "History of Music," by Professor F. L. Ritter, Vol. I.

suggest the division of the octave into twelve semitones, an innovation out of which all our modern key relationship and modulation has grown.

This change was greatly forwarded by the influence of two of Willaert's pupils, Nicolo Vincentino and Cipriano de Rore, and by still another pupil, Giuseffo Zarlino, a renowned theorist.

Other distinguished Venetian organists and harpsichordists of the sixteenth century were Claudio Merulo di Correggio, Annibale Padovano, Andrea Gabrieli and Giovanni Gabrieli, most of them pupils of Willaert, and all partakers of his ideas. They wrote *toccatas*, full of lively passages and arpeggios, calculated especially with reference to the evanescent tones of the harpsichord as contrasted with the continuous sound of the organ; *Canzoni*, in a more lyric style; and *Sonatas*, in free counterpoint.

The change to the monophonic style was a very gradual one. One of the most important agencies in effecting it, as already pointed out in a former chapter, was the invention of opera at Florence in the last half of the sixteenth century. For the first time solo singers were provided with recitatives and arias, to which was added a simple accompaniment for the harpsichord.

It soon became customary to write only a bass part for the harpsichordist or organist, the harmony being indicated by means of figures over the notes.

But the player was commonly expected not simply to play the chords indicated by the figures, but to invent an accompaniment in imitative counterpoint, and this remained the custom for more than a hundred years. The ability to do this was regarded as one of the greatest tests of musicianship.

But there was more or less of free accompaniment in simple harmony, and the transfer of the recitatives and airs to the instrument, with the accompaniment, gradually familiarized players with the idea of a monophonic instrumental style.

Still, the very ease and simplicity of it was in some sense a hindrance to its adoption. Musicians prided themselves on their ability to overcome the difficulties of elaborate counterpoint, and he who could most easily master its intricate mysteries was accounted of the highest rank in his profession. The highest tests of excellence were intellectual ones; music had not yet come to be considered primarily in its relation to emotion.

Improvisation of counterpoint.

The ability required of players was the ability to play a complex web of voice-parts interwoven according to the rules of counterpoint, and, on occasion, to invent counterpoint to a given figured bass.

Musicianship demanded of players.

Among the most renowned players and composers of this period ought to be mentioned Girolamo Frescobaldi (1588–1645 ?), said to have been an original genius, and to have written with especial reference to the capacities of the harpsichord as distinguished from the organ. He was organist at St. Peter's in Rome all the latter part of his life.

Frescobaldi 1588–1645.

His pupil, Johann Jacob Froberger (1635–1695), court organist to the Emperor Ferdinand, was the most celebrated German player of the last half of the seventeenth century. Bernardo Pasquini (1637–1710), organist at St. Mary's in Rome, occupied a similar high rank.

In England there was a school of distinguished players and contrapuntists. Thomas Tallis was organist to Queen Elizabeth in 1575, and so was his pupil, William Bird (1538–1623). Other distinguished names are those of Dr. Bull (died 1622), Orlando Gibbons (1583–1625), and especially Henry Purcell (1658–1695).

Specimens of their works are given in Weitzmann's " Geschichte " and in Burney's " History of Music." Some examples quoted by Burney from Dr. Bull are full of remarkable difficulties in the shape of passages in double thirds and sixths, some of which seem almost impossible of execution.

In France the most distinguished players and composers of this period were Jean Henry D' Anglebert, court harpsichordist to Louis XIV, and François Couperin (1668–1733), a composer of much greater importance. His pieces were polyphonic, but the upper voice-part was often the predominant melody, and all the voices were ornamented with trills, mordents, appoggiaturas, etc.

Contemporary with Sebastian Bach were Louis Marchand (1669–1732), a very distinguished player, and Jean Phillippe Rameau (1683–1764), whose work as a composer, though important, was much less significant than his labors as a theorist. He published a work on thoroughbass, *i.e.*, the science of chords and the art of harmonic accompaniment to a given voice, in which the old polyphonic standpoint was forsaken, that of monophony, the style in which one melody should be principal and the others subordinate was fairly occupied, and the ground was prepared for the development of lyric harpsichord music and of the sonata, which took place in the next generation.

In Germany, besides Froberger, already mentioned, the seventeenth century had many excellent organists and harpsichordists, among the most distinguished of whom were Hans Leo Hasler (1564-1612), born in Nuernberg, but court organist to the Emperor Rudolph II, in Vienna, a composer of very great merit; Adam Gumpeltzhaimer, Melchior Franck, Samuel Scheidt, in the first half of the century; Johann Kaspar Kerl (died 1690), Johann Pachelbel (1653-1706), George Muffat, Andreas Werckmeister, Dietrich Buxtehude (died 1707), and Friedrich Wilhelm Zachau, Haendel's teacher, in the latter half.

FROBERGER (1635-1695) deserves more extended mention, both on account of his prominence and because of his romantic adventures. He was the son of a cantor in Halle, and, showing great talent, was taken to Vienna by the Swedish ambassador, who had heard him play, and introduced to the Emperor Ferdinand III.

The Emperor became his patron, and sent him to Rome to study with Frescobaldi. After three years, having finished his studies, he went to Paris and

CHAP. XIV.

Dresden, and then, returning to Vienna, became court organist. In 1662 he received permission to visit London. He was robbed on his way through France, and, barely escaping with life, reached Calais in rags. He managed to take passage to London, but when near the English coast, the ship was taken by pirates, and he jumped overboard and swam ashore to avoid captivity or worse. Taking refuge in some fishermen's huts, they furnished him with one of their old suits, and in this guise he begged his way to London.

Becomes bellows blower in St. Paul's, London.

There he entered St. Paul's, during service, to give thanks for his deliverance. At the close of the service he was accosted somewhat roughly by the organist, who learning that he was hungry and penniless, and knowing nothing of his character as a musician, offered him the job of blowing the bellows. This Froberger accepted in his need, said nothing of his profession, and continued in his humble office until the marriage of Charles II with Catherine of Portugal. On this occasion he was so absent-minded as to let the wind out of the bellows, and the playing came to an abrupt and mortifying close in an important part of the solemnities. The organist flew at him furiously, bestowed on him some kicks and cuffs and rushed away. A lucky inspiration came to Froberger. He filled the bellows quickly, ran to the organist's bench and began to play in a style which was at once recognized by a court lady who had formerly been in Vienna. He was speedily sent for, told his strange

Becomes known by accident.

story, played before the King and his court, was received with great favor and richly rewarded.

<small>Returns to Vienna.</small>

After a while he took his departure for Vienna, but his long absence had given offence and this had been aggravated by some slanders so that he was not even admitted to the presence of the Emperor. Mortified and indignant, he sent in his resignation and withdrew to Mayence, where he passed the remainder of his days in opulence, but in ill-humor with himself and with all the world.

These names bring us to the period of Sebastian Bach, and with him to the climax of polyphonic composition for the harpsichord. But the seeds of the free lyric, monophonic style had long been sown, and, as we have seen, sprung up into luxuriant growth in the next generation.

<small>Kuhnau, 1667-1722.</small>

Even during Sebastian Bach's lifetime, signs of the approaching change were not wanting. Johann Kuhnau (1667-1722), Bach's immediate predecessor in the Cantorship of the St. Thomas School in Leipzig, did much toward laying the foundations on which Emanuel Bach built. He wrote sonatas in from three to eight movements, and strove toward a lyric style and in the direction of freeing the harpsichord from the shackles of counterpoint.

B. THE EPOCH OF THE SONATA.

<small>Viennese players.</small>

The Vienna of Mozart and Beethoven contained a group of distinguished players and composers; the Abbé Vogler, Sterkel, Wanhal, Gelinek, Pleyel,

Wolfl, Steibelt and Dussek. Their works are now obsolete, only one or two pieces of Dussek being still current.

Hummel, 1778-1837.

J. N. HUMMEL (1778-1837), a pupil of Mozart, was, in his day, considered the rival of Beethoven. He was an accomplished musician, a player of the first rank, a prolific composer, and a successful teacher. His works are now rapidly passing into oblivion.

Czerny, 1791-1857.

CARL CZERNY (1791-1857) was another Viennese celebrity; a player of high rank, a teacher of great reputation and a prolific composer of studies and pieces, mostly intended for teaching purposes.

His studies, for the most part, amplified and emphasized technical points to be met with in Clementi. The content of his pieces is never important. None of them go beyond the merely melodious and pleasing. In this he is fully in accord with the Parisian pianists, his contemporaries, Kalkbrenner, Herz, Bertiai, Huenten, *et id omne genus*, the "Philistines" against whom the Romanticists waged merciless war.

The Philistines.

Some of Clementi's pupils deserved and received much greater consideration.

Cramer, 1771-1858.

J. B. CRAMER (1771-1858) lived in England, was an excellent pianist and musician, and composed a great deal of music, none of which is now current except his famous studies.

Berger, 1777-1839.

LUDWIG BERGER (1777-1839) was Mendelssohn's teacher, and also wrote some valuable studies.

Klengel, 1783-1852.

A. A. KLENGEL (1783-1852) was a renowned

pianist and organist and cultivated mainly the polyphonic style of writing. His forty-eight canons and the same number of fugues are very learned productions.

Last, but not least, among Clementi's pupils, comes JOHN FIELD (1782–1837), who fairly ushered in the Romantic era by inventing the Nocturne, a lyric composition of a distinctly sentimental character, intended to express the various phases of feeling appropriate to the night time. They served as models for Chopin's compositions of the same name; and, although the Chopin nocturnes are vastly more significant than Field's, the resemblance was so apparent that Chopin was thought by many to have been a pupil of Field.

These nocturnes were a really original invention. In these, for the first time, the lyric sentimental element was entirely freed from all considerations of classical Form. There was no preconceived, elaborate plan; the form is the simplest possible grouping of single periods, is reduced to its lowest terms and to an entirely subordinate position; the sentiment is first and the form second. They are the fore-runners of the Songs without Words, the Ballades, Impromptus, Fantasias, in short, of the whole family of lyric pieces which began to come into vogue about the year 1830.

Field was an Irishman, born in Dublin. After studying some time with Clementi, he went with him to Russia in 1804 and spent most of the remainder of his life there. He wrote sonatas, concertos,

Field, 1782-1837.

CHAP. XIV.

Moscheles,
1794-187

and other pieces, and was one of the best pianists of his time.

One of the most prominent figures of this time was IGNAZ MOSCHELES *(1794-1870). He was born in Prague of Hebrew parents, early made the acquaintance of nearly all the best music then published, distinguished himself as virtuoso, artist and composer, played and taught a long time in London, became very intimate with Mendelssohn, with whom he was associated in the Leipzig conservatory, and continued his connection with that school until his death.

As a player.

As a player, Moscheles was celebrated for his bold and brilliant style, for the power and variety of his touch, and for his octave playing. Curiously enough, he executed octave passages with a stiff wrist.

His compositions.

As a composer he was very prolific, wrote seven great concertos, highly thought of and effective in their day, but now superseded; several sonatas, three sets of highly esteemed studies and a large number of parlor pieces which retained their popularity for a long time.

Moscheles outlived by many years the three great Romantic composers. He was well acquainted with their works, knew them all personally, and was intimately associated with two of them.

Of course his own work as a composer could not

*See " Recent Music and Musicians," by Moscheles (Henry Holt & Co., N. Y.), for an account of his own life and works. It is also a somewhat gossipy and very interesting record of his intercourse with the famous musicians of the first half of this century.

help being affected by the Romantic ideals, but he, nevertheless, remained an essentially classical composer and player in his tastes and tendencies.

He was a teacher of great reputation, and formed many players, who attained distinction.

C. THE CONTEMPORARIES OF THE ROMANTICISTS AND THEIR SUCCESSORS TO THE PRESENT.

It will be remembered that all the Romanticists, including Liszt, were born in the years 1809-11. About the same time were born a number of distinguished musicians, of a lower rank than the first, but still of no small merit.

Prominent among these is ADOLPH HENSELT (born 1814), a distinguished virtuoso, a thorough musician and a composer of marked ability. Although his compositions, so far as known to the present writer, involve no technical principles not announced and exemplified by others, yet his Etudes, op. 2 and op. 5, for example, which are among the best known of his works, emphasized certain effects in a way that stamps his style with marked individuality. These effects are especially the delivery of a melody *legato* with an accompaniment of chords to be played by the same hand, the chords being often at such a distance from the notes of the melody as makes the proper execution of these passages very difficult. He also sets a similar task for both hands simultaneously. In some of these etudes the left hand has a series of widely extended chords, the upper notes of which constitute the principal melody, while the right hand has a figured accompaniment. His master-work is his great concerto in F minor, op. 16.

Henselt has been settled in St. Petersburg since about 1837, occupied mainly in teaching.

Hiller, 1811.

Another conspicuous figure in this generation of musicians was Ferdinand Hiller, born 1811, at Frankfort-on-the-Main. Like Moscheles and Mendelssohn, he was of Jewish parentage. He was a pupil of Hummel, and occupies somewhat the same position with reference to the Romanticists that Hummel did to Beethoven, Schubert and Weber. He is a consummate musician, a respected composer, without much genius, a fine player of the classical school and an able conductor. He has been for many years director of the conservatory at Cologne.

Heller, 1815.

STEPHEN HELLER (born 1815) is a sort of miniature Chopin. He has written nothing great, but much that is refined, elegant, and within certain limits expressive. He is best known by his excellent studies in phrasing and interpretation, op. 16, 45, 46 and 47. He has been for many years a teacher in Paris.

Other good composers.

Other good composers or players or both of this generation were Th. Kullak, A. Dreyschock, Ernst Haberbier, Robert Volkman, W. Sterndale Bennett, Niels W. Gade, Louis Kœhler, Leopoid de Meyer, Fritz Spindler, Henry Litolff, Charles Hallé, Wm. Taubert, Albert Loeschorn, Carl Eckert, H. Dorn and C. F. Weitzmann, the distinguished Berlin composer, teacher, theorist and critic of Berlin, author of the History of Pianoforte Music (Geschichte des Clavierspiels und der Clavierliteratur) heretofore cited.

To a somewhat later generation belong Joachim Raff, Wm. Speidel, Ch. Lysberg, Th. Kirchner, Otto Dresel, Auguste Dupont, Otto Goldschmidt, Rich Hoffmann, Solomon Jadassohn, Louis Ehlert, Louis M. Gottschalk, H. A. Wollenhaupt, Waldemar Bargiel, Dionys Prueckner, Hans von Buelow, the two brothers Anton and Nicolaus Rubinstein, Th. Leschetizky, Ernst Pauer and Carl Reinecke.

Want of space forbids more than the mere mention of the names of most of these men. Brief notices of them may be found in Mathews' "Dictionary of Music and Musicians" (Part IX of "How to Understand Music"), and more extended accounts in Grove's Dictionary.

But at least four of them are too important or too interesting to American readers to be passed over thus lightly. These are Raff, A. Rubinstein, von Buelow and Gottschalk.

JOACHIM RAFF was born at Lachen in Switzerland, in 1822. His youth and early manhood were one long struggle with poverty, by which his education, both musical and collegiate, was greatly hindered. But he had great energy and persistence and a natural tendency to music. He supported himself by teaching and afterward by composing numerous parlor pieces for the piano. He gradually made himself a fine player and musician, and became a great master of orchestral composition. He was befriended by Liszt after the usual generous fashion of that master, and received from him encouragement and influential aid as well as valuable criticism.

His rank as composer.

Raff ranks as one of the first of living composers, and has written a large number of important works, including ten great symphonies, operas, cantatas, chamber music, concertos for different instruments with orchestra, songs, pianoforte pieces, etc. The latter are less important than most of his other works, many of them having been written down to the popular demand out of the mere necessity of making a living. They are excellent parlor pieces, however, and some of his pianoforte pieces are wholly worthy of so melodious and learned a writer. Among them there is perhaps nothing better than his pianoforte concerto, which is as fresh as it is learned and skilfully written.

Raff has been director of the Conservatory at Frankfort-on-the-Main since 1877.

Rubinstein, 1829.

ANTON GREGOR RUBINSTEIN was born in Russia, of Jewish parents, in 1829. He showed remarkable musical gifts in early childhood, studied the pianoforte in Moscow, and made his first concert tour at the age of ten years. During this tour he went to Paris, where he spent some time with Liszt. The next year he went to London and also played on the continent.

In 1845 he studied composition in Berlin, taught a couple of years in Pressburg and Vienna, and then returned to St. Petersburg, where he devoted himself to study until 1856. From that time he has been considered one of the world's greatest artists. His countrymen have heaped honors upon him, and he has rendered great services in return.

He founded the Conservatory at St. Petersburg in 1862, and was director of it for five years. Since then he has made many concert tours and has devoted much of his time to composition.

His American tour in (1872-3), gave us opportunity to admire his wonderful technic, the power and delicacy of his touch, the refinement, grace, fire, force and imagination of his playing. In most of these qualities he has never been surpassed, unless, perhaps, by Liszt.

As an interpreter of the masters, Rubinstein is somewhat erratic, seeming to treat the piece in hand as if it was an improvisation and often paying small respect to the composer's intention. His interpretations also vary with his moods.

He has been a prolific composer of piano music, songs, chamber music, etc., has written five symphonies and a number of operas and oratorios. Of all these his "Ocean" symphony holds thus far the highest acknowledged rank, and next to that his chamber music. His pianoforte music is almost all brilliant and effective and some of it is genuinely poetic. Its permanent worth is yet to be determined.

HANS GUIDO VON BUELOW was born in Dresden in 1830. His musical gifts did not appear until after a dangerous attack of brain fever, in his ninth year. He was then placed under the instruction of that most original and excellent teacher, Fr. Wieck. He afterwards studied the pianoforte with Litolff, and theory with M. K. Eberwein and Moritz Hauptmann. His parents were unwilling that he should become a professional musician, and sent him to Leipzig in 1848 to study jurisprudence at the university. The next year he was at the Berlin University, interested in politics, writing democratic articles, and musical papers defending the writings of Liszt and Wagner.

Becomes a musician.

In 1850 he finally broke with the law and went to Zuerich to have the advantage of Wagner's advice and counsel. The next year he went to Weimar to continue his pianoforte studies with Liszt, and two years later he made his first concert tour.

From 1855 to 1864 he was the leading pianoforte teacher in Stern's Conservatory at Berlin. In the latter year he went to Munich as conductor of the Royal Opera and director of the Conservatory of Music. His intimacy with Liszt and Wagner continued, and he spent part of 1866–7 with Wagner at Lucerne.

Marriage and divorce.

This friendship had a tragic ending. Von Buelow had married in 1857, Cosima, a natural daughter of Liszt by the Countess of Agoult, with whom Liszt had lived on the same terms that Chopin lived with Mme. George Sand. Mme. von Buelow seems to have inherited her parents' disregard of the obligations of the marriage tie. At any rate, after living with her husband some twelve years and bearing him five children, it occurred to her that she preferred Richard Wagner to him, and she forthwith went to live with the elder musician, taking her children with her, and with him she continued until his death.

Von Buelow procured a divorce, left Munich, and has since spent his time largely in concert tours in Europe and America. It has been repeatedly said that he was insane, an exaggeration probably occasioned by his numerous eccentricities and by the nervous excitement due to his domestic misfortunes and his overwork.

Peculiarities.

He has always been an indefatigable worker in numerous fields. His compositions are not widely known and have made little impression on the world at large. But he is an excellent conductor, a profound and accurate scholar, one of the best of editors of ancient and modern classics, and a pianist of the highest rank.

Attainments.

He has a remarkable memory, conducts a large repertoire of symphonies and operas, including the most intricate and difficult ones of Wagner, *without a score;* and plays nearly the whole range of pianoforte music from the most ancient times to the present *from memory.* No wonder if he were insane!

As a player, his technic is beyond criticism and his interpretations characterized by a consummate intelligence which includes the minutest details in all their relations. The care with which all the ideas are discriminated, each receiving its due

As a player.

proportion of emphasis, is a revelation to most players.

Withal, he is not a cold player, as some think, although he lacks the passionate *abandon* and headlong rush of Rubinstein. There is warmth and passion enough, but they are always controlled by intelligence. His concert tour in this country, made in 1874-5, two years after Rubinstein's, was very successful, and contributed much to the increase of musical appreciation and intelligence.

Gottschalk, 1829-1869.

LOUIS MOREAU GOTTSCHALK, the first American pianist, who became known all over the country by his concert tours, was born in New Orleans in 1829. He was of Creole blood.

In 1841 he went to Paris, studied with Charles Hallé and with Chopin, became a pianist of very high rank, made concert tours on the continent and returned to America in 1853. The rest of his life was spent in concert tours in North and South America. He died in Rio Janeiro in 1869.

Compositions.

He had marked originality as player and composer, but his compositions are not likely to be permanent. They are facile, fluent, and characteristic, but the feeling in them is shallow, often artificial and exaggerated, and may properly be characterized as sentimentality rather than sentiment.

Playing.

His programmes were largely made up of them to the exclusion of better things, but he was among the first to give the American public ideas of fine touch, delicacy, power and consummate ease and mastery in performance as well as of expression, within his somewhat narrow range, and so he contributed much toward laying the foundations of musical appreciation and cultivation in this country.

Of composers born since 1830, Johannes Brahms (born 1833) heads the list, followed by Camille St. Saens (1835), Adolf Jensen (1837-79), Josef Rheinberger (1839), Peter Tschaikowsky (1840), Louis Brassin (1840) and his brother Leopold, Edward Grieg (1843), Phillip Scharwenka (1847), his brother Xaver Scharwenka (1850), and Moritz Moszkowski (1853).

It is still too early to determine the permanent rank of these men, even of Brahms, who is the best known and is one of the greatest of living musicians.

He was ushered into the musical world by Schumann as a young man of the greatest promise. This promise he has at least fulfilled in large measure His two symphonies have great merits, both of composition and invention, and so have his songs, chamber-music and pianoforte-music.

His concertos are of the most difficult, combining all the technical difficulties yet invented, and showing deep marks of the influence of Schumann and hardly less of that of Liszt.

ST. SAENS is an organist and pianist of great eminence in Paris. His orchestral pieces the "Danse Macabre" and "Phaeton" are well known in this country and are among the cleverest pieces of programme music ever written. The latter, especially, so vividly reproduces the impressions made on the feelings by the successive events of the well-known myth that the story can be followed in the music without the least difficulty.

JENSEN is best known in this country by his Etudes, op. 32.

RHEINBERGER is a teacher and conductor in Munich, and has written important works in many departments.

LOUIS BRASSIN and his brother Leopold are Belgians, and both are composers of marked ability.

TSCHAIKOWSKY is teacher of composition in the Moscow Conservatory, and has shown great ability in different departments of composition. His pianoforte music includes a concerto, and is coming into constantly increasing prominence among pianists.

GRIEG is a Norwegian composer of marked originality. His sonatas and other forms involving sustained thinking and thematic development are fragmentary and weak, notwithstanding detached beauties. His strength lies in his short characteristic pieces for the pianoforte, marked by the peculiar coloring of the Scandinavian folk-music.

The two Scharwenkas are prominent teachers and composers in Berlin. The pianoforte music of both is highly esteemed and its reputation is increasing.

MOSZKOWSKI has perhaps greater genius than any of the younger generation. He lives in Berlin. His pianoforte pieces are rapidly making their way wherever music is known.

To these names must be added that of Giovanni

Sgambati, an Italian pianist and composer whose work marks an era in the history of pianoforte music in Italy. He was born in Rome in 1843. His mother was an English woman, which may account, in part, for the peculiar turn of his genius.

It may almost be said that there has been no great Italian pianist since the days of Scarlatti; for Clementi, although an Italian by birth and blood, was an Englishman in his education. Up to a very recent period, Italian music, since the rise of Italian opera, has been almost exclusively in that field; a field, too, long since thoroughly discredited in the rest of Europe by the increasing predominance of the intellectual over the sensuous element.

The musical pre-eminence long enjoyed by the Netherlanders and afterward by the Italians was transferred to Germany not long after the death of Palestrina; and there it has remained ever since.

But of late years there has been a marvelous intellectual awakening in Italy. Verdi, pre-eminent in the purely pleasing and effective style of Italian opera, produced, at an age when most composers are past learning from their opponents, his "Aida" and his Manzoni Requiem, two great works which show him to have been powerfully affected by the theories and practice of Wagner.

SGAMBATI, as pianist and composer, belongs as completely to the new school of romanticism as Brahms, the friend and disciple of Schumann. He is the one Italian pianist and composer who now enjoys a high reputation all over Europe. Before he was twenty he had become famous for his playing of Bach, Haendel, Beethoven, Chopin and Schumann. When Liszt went to Rome, about this time, Sgambati availed himself to the full of the great master's friendly advice and criticism, and became not only a great pianist, but an excellent musician, conductor and composer. He was the first to give orchestral performances in Rome of the works of the great German masters.

Composition. He has written some important orchestral works and chamber music, as well as pianoforte pieces and a concerto. This last displays most of the technical difficulties peculiar to the Romantic writers, and shows very remarkably the influence of Schumann. It has high intellectual qualities and no small emotional significance.

Besides these there are hundreds of meritorious composers whose names can not be mentioned here, for lack of space.

Lady pianists. Of the multitudes of living pianists of note only a few can be spoken of here. To give first place to the ladies : there are Marie Krebs, Madeline Schiller, Anna Mehlig and Sophie Menter, besides two in whom Americans are especially interested, Annette Essipoff and Mme. Julia Rivé-King, the former from her American tour in 1875, and the latter because she is an American by birth. Both are pianists and interpretative artists of very high rank.

Mme. Essipoff, 1853. Mme. ESSIPOFF is a Russian, born in 1853. She studied in St. Petersburg with Leschetizky, now her husband. Her playing is characterized by grace, delicacy, refinement and especially by the beautiful "coloring" she produces by her exquisite touch. She excels as an interpreter of Chopin.

Mme. Rivé-King, 1853.

Mme. RIVÉ-KING was born in Cincinnati, in 1853. Her father was a portrait painter and her mother an able teacher of the voice and the pianoforte. She showed talent very early, went to New York and studied with the well-known teacher and composer S. B. Mills, and then spent some time with Liszt in Weimar.

Since her return in 1875 she has played numerous programmes of the highest order, all over the United States and Canada, from Boston to San Francisco, and has earned a reputation of which Americans are proud. Her repertory includes the best of all schools, from Bach to Liszt and the younger composers since, and she is an admirable interpreter of the greatest works for the pianoforte. She has also composed graceful and pleasing pieces.

In 1877 she was married to Frank H. King, her manager, and now lives in New York.

Male pianists.

Of male pianists known in this country must be mentioned Franz Rummel, Constantine Sternberg, Rafael Joseffy and Wm. H. Sherwood. The two former are both pianists of high reputation.

Joseffy, 1852.

JOSEFFY is one of the greatest of living virtuosi. He is a Hungarian, born in 1852, and was a pupil of Moscheles and Tausig. His technic is unsurpassed. As an interpreter he excels in such works as require exquisite delicacy, refinement and finish, being much less successful in those which demand

CHAP. XIV.

Sherwood, 1854.

breadth, power, depth and nobility of style, He has been in this country since 1879, and has become well known.

WM. H. SHERWOOD was born in Lyons, N. Y., in 1854, and was the son of a music teacher. His talent developed early, and he went to Berlin in 1871 to study with Kullak, and afterward spent some time with Liszt.

After four years spent in Europe he returned to America and has since played in many of the cities of the United States, everywhere winning the reputation of a pianist and interpretative artist of the first rank. His technic is equal to all possible demands, and he interprets the greatest as well as the most delicate and refined compositions of all schools with the true insight of a born artist. His rendering of the Schumann "Etudes Symphoniques," the great Sonata, op. 111, and the E flat concerto of Beethoven, and the Bach Chromatic Fantasia and Fugue, are among the most satisfactory performances it has ever been the good fortune of the present writer to hear.

Mr. Sherwood has also composed several pieces of much promise.

CONCLUSION.

Our survey is now complete. We have passed in review all the important composers of pianoforte music, have analyzed their work, classified them according to the principles which governed their creative activity, and traced the development of those principles to their results in the different epochs. The technical side of pianoforte playing has been similarly treated, and composers below the first or epoch-making rank have received as much attention as the limits of the book would permit.

CONCLUSION.

In the light of this discussion we may perceive that the time in which we live belongs to the Romantic epoch. The three great romanticists died early, but their great colleague, Liszt, still lives, and it is but a few days since Richard Wagner, a greater mind than any since Beethoven, and an extreme Romanticist, was laid in his grave at Bayreuth. Wagner, to be sure, was not a pianoforte composer, but it can hardly be doubted that his indirect influence has had no small effect on all departments of musical activity and especially production. That influence is apparently on the increase, and so is that of Schumann, the most intensely romantic of pianoforte composers. The public is beginning to understand both Schumann and Wagner, and the

The present time belongs to the Romantic epoch.

Conclusion.

Romantic ideal now predominant.

tide of interest in the Romantic composers seems to be rising.

Moreover, all the rising young composers show strongly the influence of Schumann, and all are permeated with Romantic ideas. The aim of all composers of standing, nowadays, is to give worthy expression to some phase of emotional experience. Originality is shown, as in the case of Grieg, Svendsen and others, in seeking some peculiar manifestation of feeling, perhaps some national or provincial type, and giving it adequate musical embodiment. The intelligence of composers is directed, not, as in the classical epoch, to the invention of new and more elaborate forms, or to the development of existing forms to their logical limits, but to the more complete and subtle comprehension of the relation of music to feeling. Their productive work is the embodiment of the results of this increase of intelligence. There are, indeed, composers who lay great stress on the intellectual side of music as represented in Form; who write sonatas, symphonies, fugues; there are even attempts to revive the suite and the ancient dance forms. There are those, too, who emphasize the sensuous at the expense of the intellectual and emotional elements of music. But, on the whole, the Romantic ideal is dominant and its influence seems to be on the increase.

But are there tendencies discernible which are likely to produce a new revolution in pianoforte music? Is there some new ideal, conceived or conceivable, which may supplant that of the Romantic epoch as that supplanted those which preceded it?

So far as now appears, the last question must be answered in the negative. There are only three possible kinds of ideals in music: (1) those which relate to sensuous gratification, (2) those which give intellectual satisfaction, and (3) those which relate to the expression of feeling. We have already seen that the third is now dominant, and is in process of fulfillment. The second once held exclusive sway, but is now merged and absorbed in the third. The romanticists were not less but more intellectual than the classicists, but their intelligence was held subordinate to the new ideal, which they regarded as supreme. So the ideal of the Pleasing in Sensation, once supreme, has become subordinate to the intellectual and emotional elements. But at the same time, the means of sensuous gratification have been immensely enlarged, in connection with the demands of Form and expression. The resources of the modern orchestra, as developed by Wagner, Berlioz and others are vastly greater than ever existed before, and the harmonic and rhythmic additions to the resources of pianoforte composers made by Schumann and Chopin were very great.

The only progress which now seems possible is in the more perfect and complete realization of the three great ideals which have already been conceived and in great measure realized. As regards pianoforte music, the direction which improvement must take seems clear enough. The limitations of the

Conclusion.

Only three kinds of musical ideals possible.

How progress is now possible.

instrument are patent to everybody,—as patent as were the limitations of the harpsichord two centuries ago. The pianoforte produces neither a sustained tone nor an increase of power in any tone after a string has been struck. These defects will doubtless be remedied, and we may look forward to a keyed instrument which shall surpass and supplant the pianoforte, as the pianoforte surpassed and supplanted the harpsichord and the clavichord. How this will be done and how long it will take we can not say. There are those even now who are working on the problem.

It is not at all improbable that Helmholtz's well-known experiments on overtones by means of a series of tuning-forks reinforced by resonators and kept in vibration by means of electricity, may point the way to the final solution. Perhaps the coming instrument may employ tuning-forks instead of strings, and may even give the player command at will of all the varieties of tone-color producible by the orchestra. Who knows? At any rate, it seems plain that in this direction we are to look for the next great revolution in pianoforte music.

When the new instrument has been invented and perfected; when players and composers have become thoroughly familiar with its peculiarities; when some great creative genius of the first rank has devoted his powers to the production of music calculated for the new effects, then the music of Beethoven and Chopin and Schumann will be to the music of that day what Bach's music is to our own time. We shall have learned editors "translating" the *sonata appassionata* and the *etudes symphoniques* "from the language of the pianoforte into that of its modern successor," as von Buelow has done with the Bach *Chromatic Fantasia* and other harpsichord music.

But this is speculation, not history, and perhaps even wild speculation. What our successors will see it would be idle further to conjecture.

ADDENDUM.

Since this book was first published, a considerable number of young pianists and composers have become more or less known. It is, of course, not possible to mention all the meritorious ones, even if they were all known to the writer; but some of them have come to occupy so commanding a position that a brief notice of them is essential to anything like completeness. Some of them, indeed, as well as older and better known ones, really required notice in the first edition, the omission being due to the writer's comparative unfamiliarity with their work. Prominent among these must be named Dr. Louis Maas, of Boston, a pianist and composer of rare excellence. As an interpreter of great works of all schools, ancient and modern, he is extremely satisfactory. His playing is characterized by intelligence of the highest order, by breadth and nobility of style, by a vivid but chastened imagination and by a completeness of repose which sometimes passes for coldness with superficial or unsympathetic auditors. He controls passion and is never controlled by it, so that his performances have a remarkable evenness of quality. Of several severe programmes which the writer has heard him play no remembrance remains of a single detail which one could wish to have otherwise than exactly as it was. Dr. Maas was born in

Wiesbaden, Germany, in 1852, but spent his youth in London, whither his family removed. He was a pupil of the Leipzig Conservatory from 1867 to 1871 and a teacher in the same institution from 1875 to 1880. Since the latter date he has been established in Boston. He has written symphonies and chamber music, besides music for his instrument, and many of his works are highly spoken of. Most of them the writer has had no opportunity to hear.

Other Boston pianists and composers who have acquired reputation national in its extent are Arthur Foote, Geo. W. Chadwick, B. J. Lang, Carlyle Petersilea, Edw. B. Perry, Ernst Perabo, Carl C. Baermann, Mrs. Anna Steiniger-Clark, and Carl Faelten. The two former are known outside of Boston mainly by their compositions. Both have written pianoforte works, chamber and orchestral music of no small degree of merit and have made the American composer respected in Europe.

Mme. Teresa Carreño is a concert-pianist of the most brilliant type. As an interpreter of most masters she is open to the charge of modifying the composer's intention to suit her own fancy, changing the embellishments, cadences and introductions of Chopin's pieces, for example, in a way not to be approved by a conscientious critic. But the tropical fervor of her imagination, the fire, force and electric brilliancy of her performances never fail to excite an audience to the highest pitch of enthusiasm. Her playing of Liszt and of other brilliant composers is especially successful and effective.

She was born in Venezuela in 1853, of a distinguished Spanish family. She showed her gifts in early childhood, received her first lessons from her father, and later studied with Gottschalk in New York. Her home is now in the latter city, whence she makes concert tours in both North and South America.

Mr. Albert R. Parsons, of New York, is an excellent pianist, but is known outside of that city mainly through his translation of Wagner's essay on Beethoven, his work as an editor of pianoforte music for teaching purposes and his reputation as a teacher. He belongs among the most thoughtful, able and intelligent of American musicians.

Philadelphia is represented in the ranks of concert pianists first and foremost by Mr. Charles H. Jarvis, who first became known west of the Alleghanies by his admirable recital at the Indianapolis meeting of the Music Teachers' National Association in 1887. His programme, beginning with the Beethoven *Sonata appassionata*, included a wide range of style and proved him an excellent interpretative artist. He was born in Philadelphia in 1837 and, as pianist and teacher, has done much to raise the standard of musical intelligence in his native city.

Mr. W. W. Gilchrist, also of Philadelphia, has written some of the best chamber music for piano and strings yet produced in this country, besides choral music. He was born in New Jersey, in 1846, and has been long settled in Philadelphia as organist and chorus director. Mr. Richard Zeckwer, Director of the Philadelphia Musical Academy, Anthony Stankowitch and Mr. John F. Himmelsbach are also excellent pianists.

Mr. Richard Burmeister and Mr. Alexander Lambert are concert pianists of marked ability. The former lives in Baltimore and the latter is director of a Conservatory of Music in New York City. Mr. Ad M. Foerster is a composer of meritorious pianoforte and chamber music. His home is in Pittsburg, Pa. Mr. Wilson G. Smith, of Cleveland, has written a considerable number of graceful pianoforte pieces.

Chicago possesses a number of concert pianists of great merit. Mme. Fanny Bloomfield-Zeisler is an artist of rare intelligence, and her playing is always characterized by great fire, force and delicacy. She was a pupil of Leschetizky. Miss Neally Stevens studied several years under the best artists in Germany, including Liszt, von Bülow, Theo. Kullak, Moszkowski and Xaver Scharwenka, and her playing fully bears out the encomiums she received from them. Miss Amy Fay is most widely known by her very interesting book, "Music Study in Germany," in which she gives an account of her experience as a pupil of Liszt, Tausig, Kullak, Deppe and others. She gives "piano-conversations" in various parts of the country. Mme. Eugenie de Roode Rice may properly be mentioned among Chicago pianists, although she has now removed to New York. She is an excellent interpreter of widely varied styles. Mr. Emil Liebling and Mr. Fred Boscovitz are the leading male pianists of Chicago. They, with Silas G. Pratt, have written a good deal of pianoforte music.

Among the very best of the young generation of American composers for the piano must be mentioned E. A. McDowell, Arthur Bird, Edgar S. Kelley and Johann H. Beck. All of them have produced excellent works and give promise of still better.

QUESTIONS.

INTRODUCTION.

When, where, and by whom was the pianoforte invented?

What instruments preceded it?

Tell how the tones were produced in each of the three instruments.

Why were the strings of the older instruments thin and light?

When did the pianoforte finally supplant them and come into general use?

CHAPTER I.

Define the terms " Melody," "Harmony," " Counterpoint," " Monophonic," " Polyphonic."

Describe the difference between Monophonic and Polyphonic Music.

What device secures *Unity* in composition?

What are the two principal kinds of strict imitation?

Describe a Canon.

Give an outline of a fugue.

Describe free imitation.

Describe the " Suite."

CHAPTER II.

Name the three greatest composers of Polyphonic music.

Give Dates.

Give a brief account of the life and work of each, omitting unimportant details.

(The author recommends that students try to remember, in the biographies, only such leading points as these: Parentage, early situation and surroundings, the same in youth, most powerful influences affecting character and development, leading personal traits, work accomplished.)

CHAPTER III.

Give examples of monophonic tendencies during the polyphonic period.
Describe the Sonata, as a whole.
What is meant by "Form" in music?
Define the terms "Period," "Section," "Phrase," "Motive," "Period Group."
How are these elements combined so as to produce a whole characterized by Unity, Variety and Symmetry?
Give plan of "Sonata Form."

CHAPTER IV.

What three composers developed the Sonata form to its logical limits?
Give Dates.
Give brief accounts of each.
Give difference between the sonatas of D. Scarlatti and those of C. P. E. Bach.
Recapitulate the essential characteristics of the modern Sonata.
How many of these were known before Emanuel Bach's time?
What did he do that had not been done before?
What did Haydn and Mozart do that had not been done before?

CHAPTER V.

What is meant by "Content" in music?
What can music express, and what can it *not* express?
What do words *express*, and what can they *suggest*?
What can music do in the way of suggesting *ideas* or expressing them *indirectly*?
Illustrate. What is a musical idea?
What is musical thinking?

How many kinds of Beauty are there in music?
How many kinds of activity are possible to the human mind?
Give examples of simple and complex feelings.
Tell the difference between desires and affections.
Describe the relation of music to feeling.
What music ranks highest, and what lowest?

Chapter VI.

Give brief account of Beethoven's life and work.
Give an approximate list of his compositions, the most important.
What gives him his prominent rank as a composer?

Chapter VII.

In what senses is the term "classic" used?
What is meant by the term "romantic"?
Give the characteristic difference between the two styles of music.

Chapter VIII.

Give brief accounts of the life and work of Weber and Schubert.
In what sense is the work of each "romantic"?
What are the marks of romanticism in Schubert's work?

Chapter IX.

Who were the three greatest romantic composers for the pianoforte?
Give brief biography of each, with year of birth and death.
Compare their characters and works.

Chapter X.

Describe the technic of the first classical period, as regards touch, sonority of instruments, demands on fingers and execution, embellishments, fingering, etc.
State the distinction between a "virtuoso," and an interpretative artist.

Chapter XI.

What advances in Technic were made by E. Bach, Haydn and Mozart?
Give difference between Viennese and English pianofortes.
Give account of Clementi's life and work.

Chapter XII.

Give account of growth of technic from Mozart to the Romantic writers.
Who developed the use of the pedal?

Chapter XIII.

Give account of the technic of the romantic composers.
Of Liszt and his work.
Give summary.
Give work of Tausig and of Dr. Wm. Mason.

INDEX.

Affections, 66-7.
Agoult, Countess of, 226.
Aida, opera by Verdi, 231.
Albrechtsberger, relations to Beethoven, 77-8.
Anglebert, J. H. d', 214.
Arpeggios peculiar to Chopin, their fingering, 198, 206.
Artists, formerly dependent on the patronage of nobles, 49, 53; contrasted with virtuosi, 185.
Bach, J. S. his life, 14-17; as a composer and player, 17, 18; his works and style, 17-19, 29, 30, 39, 41-46, 97.
Bach, C. P. E. his life, 38, 39; his music and playing, 39-41; what he did for the Sonata, 41-48.
Ballads, Chopin's, 153-4.
Bargiel, W., 223.
Beauty in music, 62, 71; Chopin's love of, 156.
Bebung, the, 189.
Beethoven, his life 72-81, 85, 86, 92-94; compositions, 75, 89-92; content and character of his music, 80-82, 85-89, 93, 99-101.
Bennett, W. S. 222.
Berger, L. 218.
Bertini, 218,
Bird, Wm. 214.
Brahms, Johannes 229; influence of Schumann on his technic, 199.
Brassin, Louis 229.
" Leopold 230; technic shows influence of Schumann, 199.
Buelow, Hans von, 223-227.
Bull, Dr., 214.

Burney's History of Music, 214.
Buxtehude, 215; visited by Bach, 15.
Canon, 9, 10.
Canzoni, 212.
Chopin, his history, 134-152; 154-156; his playing, 137, 138, 147-149; compositions, 139-141, 143, 153-156.
Classic, the, in music, 57, 58; 95-98; classic qualities in Mendelssohn, 132-3; persistence of classical technic, 196.
Clavichord, the, 2-3; its technic, 184-5.
Clementi, Muzio, 191-4.
Clinging touch, 197.
Complex feelings, 65.
Composition an intellectual process, 61.
Concertos, form of, 31; Bach's, 46; Mozart's, 188, 190; Mendelssohn's, 129; Chopin's, 139-141, 153; Schumann's, 172-3; Beethoven's, 193; Raff's, 224; Brahm's, 229; Sgambati's, 232.
Concert Stueck, Weber's, 112.
Content of music, 59-71, 97, 98; Beethoven's, 80-82, 86, 87, 93, 99; Haydn's 82-85, 99; Haendel's oratorios, 23, 24; of Bach's Passion music, 24; of Mozart's, 57, 82-85, 99; of Chopin's, 154-156; of Mendelssohn's, 131-134; of Schumann's, 65-68, 175-8; of Schubert's, 115-118; of Weber's, 111-12, 122; of Liszt's, 201-3.
Correggio, Claudio, Merulo di, 212.

Counterpoint, 7-10; double, 11.
Couperin, F., 214.
Cramer, J. B., 218.
Creation, oratorio by Haydn, 50-1.
Cristofori, invented pianoforte, 1, 3.
Czerny, C., 218.
Daily Studies, Tausig's, 207.
Danse Macabre, by St. Saens, 229.
Danzi, conductor at Stuttgart, 106.
Der Freischuetz, Opera by Weber, 109, 110.
Desires, 65.
Divisions of the Sonata Form, 34, 35, 42, 43.
Dorn, H., 222.
Dresel, Otto, 223.
Dreyschock, A., 222.
Dudevant, Aurora (George Sand), 150-1.
Dupont, A., 223.
Dussek, J. L., 218.
Ecclesiastical Keys, 211.
Eckert, C., 222.
Ehlert, L., 223.
Ehrlich, H., 217.
Elaboration in the Sonata-Form, 35.
Elijah, oratorio by Mendelssohn, 130.
Elsner, Chopin's teacher, 136, 145.
Emphasis, discriminative, impossible on harpsichord, 184; better on clavichord, 184; developed to its extreme limit by Liszt, 201-2; Romantic school demands it especially, 206.
Erl-King, song by Schubert, 114, 117.
Ernestine von Fricken, friend of Schumann, 169, 170.
Essipoff, Annette, 232-3.
Esterhazy, Prince, Haydn's patron, 49, 50; Mozart's, 49.

Ethical element in Beethoven, 87-8, 99; lacking in Chopin, 155-6.
Eugene, Prince of Wuertemberg, patron of Weber, 105.
Euryanthe, opera by Weber, 109, 110.
Exposition of a Fugue, 42.
Fantasias of early composers, 211; Mozart's in C minor, 118; Bach's Chromatic Fantasia, 19.
Feelings, 63-7, 71.
Field, John, 219.
Fingering, 183-4; 196-8 (See Technic).
Form, 31-6, 96; in Scarlatti's Sonatas, 30, 41-46; in J. S. Bach's, 30, 46; in C. P. E. Bach's, 30, 44-7; in Haendel's Suites, 46; Haydn's Sonata-forms, 51-2, 82; Mozart's, 57, 58, 82, Beethoven's, 82, 86, 87.
Franck, M., 215.
Frederick the Great, 16, 38, 39.
French Composers, 214.
Frescobaldi, 218.
Froberger, S., 13, 215-17.
Fugue, 10, 11, 16, 39.
Gabrieli, Andrea, 212.
———, Giovanni, 212.
Gade, N. W., 222.
Gaensbacher, friend of Weber, 104-5.
Gelinek, 217.
Gibbons, Orlando, 214.
Gladkowska, Constantia, relations to Chopin, 139, 149.
Glissando, octaves, in Weber's Concertstueck, 194.
Goldschmidt, O., 223.
Gottschalk, L. M., 228-29.
Gradus ad Parnassum, Clementi's, 192-4.
Grieg, E., 230.
Gumpeltzhaimer, A., 215
Haberbier, E. 222.

INDEX.

Haendel, G. F., life and works, 19-24; monophonic tendencies, 29, 30, 43, 44; form of the Suites, 46; his technic, 185.
Halle, Chas., 222, 228.
Harmony, 7.
Harpsichord, the, 2-4; its technic, 181-4.
Hasler, H. L., 215.
Haydn, F. J., biography, 47-52; compared with Mozart, 57; connection with Beethoven, 76, 77; compositions, 50-52, 82-5; his technic, 188.
Heller, Stephen, 222.
Henselt, Adolph, 121-3.
Henschkel, J. P., 103.
Hiller, F., 222.
Hoffmann, R., 223.
Hummel, J. N., 218.
Huenten, 218.
Ideals in music, 62, 237.
Ideas in music, 61.
Images, how expressed, 54, 60.
Imitation, strict, 9, 10; free, 11, 12.
Intellect, defined, 63.
Intellectual appreciation of music, 61, 67, 231.
"Invitation to Dance," 112, 122.
Italian music, 231.
" opera, Haendel's, 21-3.
Jadassohn, S., 223.
Jensen, A., 229, 230.
Joseffy, R., 233-4.
Kalkbrenner, F., 144-5, 218.
Kerl, J. K., 215.
King, F. H., 233.
Kirchner, T., 223.
Klengel, A. A., 218.
Koehler, L., 222.
Krebs, Marie, 232.
Kreisleriana, 170.
Kuhnau, J., 217.
Kullak, T., 222.

Lassus, Orlandus, 9.
Leschetizky, T., 223.
Liszt, sketch of, 199-205; works, 201-204; technic, 202, 204-5.
Liszt, Cosima, 226-7.
Litolff, H., 222.
Loeschorn, A., 222.
Ludwig, Duke of Stuttgart, 106.
Lysberg, C., 223.
Manzoni Requiem, by Verdi, 231.
Marchand, L., 212.
Martini, Padre, 54.
Mason, Wm., 208.
Mathews, W. S. B., 71, 208.
Mazurkas, Chopin's, 153-4.
Mehlig, Anna, 232.
Melody, defined, 7; form of, 31.
Mendelssohn, life of, 125-130; works, 126-131, 134; his technic, 197.
Menter, Sophie, 232.
Mental Activity, 63.
Monophonic Music, 78, 29, 31, 39-40.
Moods, simple emotions, 65.
Morzin, Count, 48-9.
Moscheles, J., 218-19.
Moszkowski, 229, 230.
Motives, 33.
Mozart, life of, 52-57; as a composer, 57-8; compared with Beethoven, 74-5, 82; content of his music, 83-5; his technic, 198-190.
Muffat, G., 215.
Music, suggests scenes, 60, 163, 165-6, 229; relation to emotion, 69.
"Oberon," by Weber, 109-110.
Operas, 21-3; 56, 92, 109, 110, 212, 231.
Oratorios, 16, 22, 23, 50, 130.
Organ music for harpsichord, 181, 211; fugues of Bach, 16, 39.
Ornaments, necessity of, 182.

252 INDEX.

Pachelbel, J., 215.
Padovano, A., 212.
Paganini, 201-2.
Palestrina, 9.
Papillons, Schumann, 163, 165-6.
Partitas of Bach, 46.
Passion Music, Bach's, 16, 17, 24; revival by Mendelssohn, 127.
Pasquini, B., 214.
Pauer, E. 223.
Pedal, use of, 194.
Periods, defined, 32.
Period groups, 33.
"Perpetual Motion," Weber, 112.
Pfeiffer, Beethoven's teacher, 73.
"Phæton," by St. Saens, 229.
Phrases, defined, 32.
"Philistines," 170-1, 218.
Pianoforte, construction, 3; technic, 218; powers, 237-38.
Pleyel, 217.
Polonaises, Chopin's, 153-5.
Polyphonic Music, 7-13.
Preludes, Chopin's, 152.
Programme Music, St. Saens, 229; Berlioz, 201.
Prueckner, D., 223.
Purcell, Henry, 212.
Quartets, form of, 31.
Quintets, form of, 31.
Raff, Joachim, 223-4.
Rameau, J. P., 214.
Reinecke, C., 223.
Rhapsodies, Liszt's Hungarian, 201.
Rheinberger, J., 229, 230.
Rhythms, of Schumann, 198-9.
Ricercari, 211.
Ries, Franz, Beethoven's violin teacher, 78.
Rigoletto, Liszt's, 202-3.
Rivé-King, Mme. Julia, 223.
Ritter's History of Music, 211.

Romantic, ideal defined, 96, 99-101; characteristics of Chopin, 136-37, 139-41, 152-56; of Mendelssohn, 126-28, 131-4; of Schumann, 159, 162, 165-70, 175-8; of Schubert, 116-19, 122; of Mozart, 118; of Bach, 19; of Weber, 109-12, 122; of Liszt, 200-1; tendencies, 235-6.
Rondo in E flat, op. 62, Weber, 112.
Rore Cipriano di, 212.
Rubinstein, N., 223.
Rubinstein, Anton, 224-25.
Rummel, Franz, 223.
Sand, George, Mme., 150-1.
Scarlatti, A., 24.
Scarlatti, Domenico, 24, 25, 30, 41-44; his technic, 187.
Scharwenka, P., 229, 230.
      " X., 229, 230.
Scheidt, S., 215.
Scherzos, Chopin's, 153-4.
Schiller, Madeline, 232.
Schubert, Franz, life, 112-14; works, 113-19.
Schumann, life, 156-174; music, 163-6, 168-9, 172; compared with Mendelssohn and Chopin, 175-8; his technic, 198-9; increasing influence, 235.
Seasons, the, Haydn's, 50.
Sections, 32.
Sensibility, defined, 63.
Sgambati, 230-2, 199.
Sherwood, W. H., 234.
Simple Emotions, 64-5.
Sonatas, Bach's, 30, 46; C. P. E. Bach's, 41-8; Scarlatti's, 30, 41-4; Haydn's, 51-2, 82; Mozart's, 57-8, 82; Beethoven's, 82-8; Kuhnau's, 217; of the 16th century, 212.
Sonata-Form, 31, 35.
Speidel, Wm., 223.
Spinet, 4.

Spindler, F., 222.
Steibelt, D., 218, 89-90.
Sternberg, C., 233.
Sterkel, 217.
Stretto, in a fugue, 11.
"St. Paul," Mendelssohn's, 130.
St. Saens, C., 229, 230.
Stuttgart, in Weber's time, 106.
Subjects, 35, 42-3.
Suites, 12, 45-6.
Symphony, form of, 31; Beethoven's "Eroica," 86, 92, Ninth, 86, 93; Schubert's, in C, 115; unfinished, in B, 115; Tragic, 114; Rubinstein's "Ocean," 225; Brahms', 229; Sgambati's, 231; Mendelssohn's 128-9
Symmetry, 32.
Tallis, Thomas, 214.
Taubert, W., 222.
Tausig, Carl, 207.
Technic, of the first classical period, 181-7; J. S. Bach's, 184-5; Haendel's, 185; Scarlatti's, 187; of the second classical period, 188-192; Mozart's, 188-90; Clementi's, 191-4; of the transition period, 193; Beethoven, 193: Schubert and Weber, 194; of the Romanticists, 194-6, Mendelssohn's, 197; Chopin's, 197; Schumann's, 198-9; Liszt's, 201-2; minor, 205-8.
Thalberg, S., 194.

Toccatas, 212.
Transitions, 35.
Trio or Alternative (Form), 34.
Tschaikowsky, P., 229, 230.
Two-finger exercise, Mason's, 208.
Unity, 32-4.
Van den Eeden, 73.
Variety, 32.
Verdi, 231.
Vincentino, Nicolo, 212.
Virginals, 4.
Virtuoso vs. Artist, 181.
Vogler, Abbé, 104, 217.
Volkmann, R., 222.
Von Breuning family, 74.
Wagner, 226, 227, 235.
Waldstein, Count, 74.
"Wanderer," by Schubert, 114.
Wanhal, 217.
Weber, Carl Maria; life, 102-9; his compositions, 107-12, 122.
Weitzman, C. F., 222.
Werkmeister, B., 215.
Wieck, Fr., 162-4, 170-1, 226.
Wieck, Clara, 162-3, 169-70, 173.
Will, 63.
Willaert, A., 211.
Woelfl, 89-90, 218.
Wollenhaupt, H. A., 223.
Wrist Action, 206-7.
Zachau, 215.
Zambona, 72.
Zarlino, C., 212.

CELEBRATED
PIANISTS

OF THE

PAST AND PRESENT.

ILLUSTRATED

With One Hundred and Fifty Portraits of European and American Pianists of the Past and Present.

HANDSOMELY AND DURABLY BOUND IN CLOTH, WITH GOLD STAMP.

PRICE $2.00.

This Volume is prepared with the utmost care, and forms one of the most reliable works on musical biography published. The American Edition contains about 50 pages of new material relating to pianists of America. This portion of this work has been carefully done. The work is very attractive in style and suitable for a gift book.

www.ingramcontent.com/pod-product-compliance
Lightning Source LLC
Chambersburg PA
CBHW032144230426
43672CB00011B/2442